# Food, Family, and Friendships

## A Collection of Favorite Memories and Memorable Favorites

*Compiled and Written by*
Mary Moss Darden and Margaret Taylor Proffitt

*Cover and Illustrations by*
Jennifer Taylor Proffitt

*Additional Artwork by*
Stewart Darden Mauldin
and Michelle Taylor Wilson

Darden & Proffitt
P.O.Box 8743
Virginia Beach, VA 23450
e-mail HOOK1UP@aol.com

Tenth Printing -September 2001

International Standard Book Number 0-9654643-1-8

Printed by
G & R
Publishing Co.
507 Industrial Street
Waverly, IA 50677

# DEDICATION

When my mother's recipe collection, which included my grandmother's recipes, came into my possession, I was concerned that the recipes would be packed away and forgotten. It was important to me that the recipes and memories be preserved. Family mealtimes at our house were relaxed and pleasant times — usually around the dining room table or on the screened porch overlooking the Pamlico River when the weather was warm. Mother liked to entertain and was a gracious hostess. I am dedicating this book to my mother, Mary S. Moss, in loving memory for all that she taught me, both in the kitchen and out.

A special thanks also to my co-author and dear friend, Margaret, without whom this book would not have become a reality.

*Mary Moss Darden*

This book is tangible evidence of the remarkable spirit and energy of family and friends, past and present. It is dedicated to them.

Having Mary as a close friend is a privilege that I treasure. Because of her, working on this book has been a joy and delight.

*Margaret Taylor Proffitt*

# APPRECIATION

The encouragement supplied to us by our families — especially by our husbands — and our friends has been of prime importance to us in the completion of this book. We appreciate their confidence in us.

The illustrations depict locations that hold special memories; the cover arrangement includes an old family china pattern from which the floral design within the book is taken. For keeping our family sentiments in mind as they produced the art work, we thank Jennifer Taylor Proffitt, Michelle Taylor, and Stewart Darden Mauldin — family members all.

We also thank Pam Feese, who took us places in our computer we would have never dared to go on our own; our good friend, Sharon Haring, who cheerfully proofread copy; and Sue Buchannan, a veteran cookbook editor, who gave us the courage to begin.

Our sincere appreciation also goes to other family members and friends, both past and present, who so readily shared recipes and, in their own ways, gave help and encouragement all along the way.

Special thanks
to the staff
at
G & R Publishers

# INTRODUCTION

F riendship brought about the beginning of this cookbook, and friendship saw it through. The two of us have been friends for many years and have at times been mistaken for sisters. Indeed, during the years that we taught in the same school, one as librarian and one as music specialist, students regularly mistook one of us for the other. Though we are not related, we have always had similar thoughts and feelings about many things.

Through the years, we often spoke of our families and their roots in North Carolina and Virginia. The fond memories we shared of foods, families, and friendships created a logical progression to talk of recipes and cookbooks. We hope the sentiments that brought us to completing this cookbook will provide you with many hours of pleasure and that its recollections will arouse your own memories of times and people special in your own lives. We hope you will feel the warmth we have felt while lovingly creating this book.

 Most of the recipes have been prepared and tasted by one or both of us. Some have come to us highly recommended by family members and friends, and we feel confident in offering those to you. The recipes following the granny faces are quite old, and some are included only because we are charmed by their wording and find them to be quite entertaining. Some of the "grannies" are so highly loaded with fat that no health-conscious cook would prepare them. On the other hand, some recipes noted by the granny face are quite healthful and can readily be followed without guilt. Those judgments are left to you.

We have tried to be somewhat consistent in the names and spellings of the ingredients but have chosen to leave many recipes worded exactly as we received them. By presenting them this way, we think they retain more of the personalities of the wonderful cooks who shared them with us. We hope you agree.

# TABLE OF CONTENTS

# Breads

Old Princess Anne County Court House

*Records of my ancestors dating back to the 1600's can be found
in the court house. I feel my roots are firmly planted here.
— M.P.*

# BREADS

## Sourdough Bread

**Starter:**

| | | | |
|---|---|---|---|
| 1 3/4 | cups unsifted, strong bread-type flour | 1 | Tablespoon sugar |
| | | 1 | Tablespoon salt |
| 1 | package active dry yeast | 2 1/2 | cups warm water |

Combine flour, sugar, salt, and yeast in large bowl. Gradually add warm water; beat 2 minutes on medium speed of mixer. Cover; let stand at room temperature (approximately 80 degrees) for 4 days. Stir down daily.

**Bread:**

| | | | |
|---|---|---|---|
| 5 to 6 | cups unsifted, strong bread-type flour, divided | 3 | Tablespoons sugar |
| | | 1 | teaspoon salt |
| 1 | package active dry yeast | 1 | cup milk |
| 2 | Tablespoons margarine | 1 1/2 | cups starter |

Combine 1 cup flour, sugar, salt, and yeast in large bowl. Place milk and margarine in saucepan over low heat until liquid is warm. Margarine does not need to melt. Gradually add to dry ingredients and beat 2 minutes at medium speed. Add starter and 1 cup flour, or enough to make thick batter. Beat at high speed 2 minutes; stir in enough flour to make soft dough. Turn onto lightly floured board, and knead until smooth and elastic. Place in greased bowl, turning to grease top. Cover; let rise in warm place about 1 hour. Punch dough down; turn out onto lightly floured board. Cover, and let rest 15 minutes. Divide dough in half; shape into 2 loaves, and place in loaf pans. Cover; let rise in warm place about 1 hour. Bake in 400 degree oven 30 minutes or until done. Remove pans and cool on racks. Makes 2 loaves.

**To replenish starter:**
Add 1 1/2 cups strong bread-type flour and 1 cup warm water to leftover starter. Beat until smooth. Cover, and let sit in warm place for 12 hours. Store in refrigerator until needed.

# Onion Sourdough Bread

| | |
|---|---|
| 1 1/2 cups sourdough starter | 3 cups unsifted bread flour, divided |
| 3 Tablespoons sugar | |
| 2 1/2 teaspoons salt | 1 package active dry yeast |
| 1 cup milk | 2 Tablespoons margarine |
| cornmeal | 1 egg white |
| 1 Tablespoon water | 2/3 cup finely chopped onion |
| caraway seeds | |

Combine 1 cup flour, sugar, salt, and undissolved yeast in a large bowl. In a saucepan, combine milk and margarine over low heat until liquid is very warm (120 to 130 degrees). Margarine does not need to melt. Gradually add to dry ingredients, and beat 2 minutes at medium speed of mixer. Add 1 1/2 cups starter and 1/4 cup flour. Beat at high speed for 2 minutes. Stir in enough additional flour to make soft dough. Turn out onto lightly floured board; knead until smooth and elastic, 8 to 10 minutes. Place in greased bowl, turning to grease top. Cover; let rise until doubled in bulk, about 1 hour. Punch dough down; turn out onto lightly floured board. Divide in half. Cover; let rest 15 minutes. Divide dough into quarters, form into round balls, and flatten slightly. Place on greased baking sheets that have been sprinkled with corn-meal. Cover; let rise until doubled. Combine egg white and water; brush over loaves, and top with chopped onion and caraway seeds. Bake at 400 degrees about 25 minutes or until done. Cool on wire racks.

# Classic White Bread

Although my husband, Don, most enjoys working with sourdough bread, he is not afraid to experiment with bread recipes of all kinds, old and new. He carries on a long-established family tradition: his mother baked excellent bread and rolls as does his sister, Janie. She and Don often share recipes and helpful hints. Our youngest son has developed bread-making skills of his own, so it seems the family tradition will continue uninterrupted. M.P.

| | | | |
|---|---|---|---|
| 1 1/2 | packages active dry yeast | 5 to 6 | cups flour (plain), sifted |
| 2 1/4 | cups milk | 3 | Tablespoons sugar |
| 2 | Tablespoons shortening | 2 | teaspoons salt |

Combine yeast and 2 1/2 cups flour. In a saucepan, heat milk, shortening, salt and sugar until warm, stirring occasionally to melt shortening. Add warm liquid mixture to dry mixture in mixing bowl. Beat at low speed 1/2 minute, scraping sides of bowl. Beat 3 minutes at high speed. By hand, stir in enough of remaining flour to make a moderately stiff dough. Turn out onto a lightly floured surface. Knead until smooth and satiny, about 8 to 10 minutes. Shape into a ball. Place in lightly greased bowl, turning once to grease surface. Cover bowl, and let dough rise in warm place until double in size, about 1 1/4 hours. Punch down; then cut dough into 2 portions. Shape each portion into a smooth ball. Cover, and let rest for 10 minutes. Shape into loaves; place into 2 greased 9x5x3-inch loaf pans. Cover, and let rise until double, about 45 to 60 minutes. To determine if bread is ready to bake, lightly press fingertips into raised dough. If indentation remains, dough is ready. Bake at 400 degrees for 35 minutes. Cover with aluminum foil if top browns too quickly. To determine if baked bread is done, lightly tap bread — will sound hollow if done.

# Salt-Rising Bread

Salt-rising bread is not easy to make. Some say the success of the bread depends on how strong the aroma of the starter is — the worse the smell, the better the bread. In our house, there have been some successes and some failures, but the unique flavor of this bread makes it worth the effort. I have seen several different recipes for salt-rising bread; this one was used by my husband's grandmother. Like many cooks of her day, she did not give very detailed cooking directions. M.P.

**Starter:**

|   |   |   |   |
|---|---|---|---|
| 4 | Tablespoons corn meal | | pinch soda |
| 1 to 2 | teaspoons sugar | 1/2 | cup milk, or a little more |

Mix dry ingredients. Heat milk to scalding; pour over cornmeal mixture. Put in warm place; let sit overnight. If it smells awful in the morning, continue with the recipe. If there is no odor, pour the mixture out and start again.

**Bread:**

|   |   |   |   |
|---|---|---|---|
| | starter | 1 | pint milk |
| | flour | 1 | teaspoon salt |
| 1 | Tablespoon sugar | | |

Scald milk. Let cool somewhat. While the milk is still good and warm, drop the starter into it. Sift enough flour to make a good batter, and place bowl in a pot of warm water. When batter rises, mix salt and sugar with enough flour to make a dough that will knead well. Put in loaf pan, and bake for 1 hour 20 minutes in a 350 degree oven.

*Augusta Jane Hogan, Lynch Station, Virginia*

# Janie's Hot Rolls

Here they are! Rolls from one of the world's best cooks. I don't promise that yours will be as good as hers, because even though you will be using her recipe, I must tell you that she truly has a special touch. Nonetheless, I'll bet her touch rubs off on you. M. P.

| | | | |
|---|---|---|---|
| 1 | Tablespoon salt | 1 | Tablespoon sugar |
| 1/2 | cup Crisco oil | 3 | cups hot water |
| 1 | Tablespoon sugar | 1 | cup milk |
| 1 | envelope active dry yeast | | flour, sifted |

In a large bowl, combine salt, 1 tablespoon sugar, oil, and hot water. Set aside. In a small saucepan, combine 1 tablespoon sugar and milk; heat until good and lukewarm. Remove from heat, sprinkle yeast on top, and set aside. Add enough flour to the water mixture to absorb all of the moisture. Add yeast mixture to large bowl, and again add enough flour to absorb the moisture. The dough should be sticky but still dry enough to handle. Turn out onto a floured board, and knead. Grease bowl. Return dough to greased bowl; cover and let rise until it has doubled in bulk. Fold dough from outside in; cover, and let double in bulk again. Form into loaves and/or rolls. This amount of dough will make 2 loaves and 1/2 dozen or more rolls. Bake in 425 degree oven for 20 to 25 minutes or until golden brown. Take up some butter or margarine on a paper towel and rub onto the tops of the loaves and rolls.

*Janie Proffitt Flippo, Roanoke, Virginia*

# Delmonico Rolls

Warm one ounce of butter in a pint of milk; put to it a spoonful and a half of yeast of small beer and a little salt; put two pounds of flour in a pan and mix with the above; let it rise an hour. Knead well and bake in a hot oven.

# Strawberry Bread

My brother, Harry, and his wife, Jean, often host a huge Christmas Eve party at their home. The decorations are always lovely and tastefully done. Jean keeps her eye out for new treats, and shared this one with me some years ago when I yelled for help at the last minute. M.P.

| | |
|---|---|
| 1 10-ounce package strawberries or 1 cup | 2 eggs |
| | 1/2 cup oil |
| 1 1/2 cups flour (plain) | 1 cup sugar |
| 1 teaspoon cinnamon | 1/2 teaspoon baking soda |
| 1/2 teaspoon salt | |

Purée strawberries and combine with eggs and oil. Whisk. Sift dry ingredients together before adding to strawberry mixture. Mix with a wooden spoon. Pour into a greased loaf pan. Sprinkle with a spoonful of sugar. Bake at 325 degrees for 1 hour and 10 minutes. Put on side to cool.

*Jean Jordan Taylor, Virginia Beach, Virginia*

# Morehead City Hush Puppies

The mention of Morehead City or Atlantic Beach to almost anyone who grew up in Eastern North Carolina will probably stimulate a discussion of summer visits to the beach. No discussion would be complete without mentioning the wonderful hush puppies. M.D.

| | |
|---|---|
| 1 pound water ground cornmeal | 2 Tablespoons sugar |
| | 1 Tablespoon salt |
| 1 egg, beaten | 1/2 pint buttermilk |
| 1/2 teaspoon soda | |

Mix all ingredients. Add water as needed. Drop by spoonful into deep pot of hot grease. Cook until brown. Remove, and drain on absorbent paper.

# Rye and Indian Muffins

Two cups of Indian meal, two cups of rye flour, half a cup of yeast. Let it rise overnight; in the morning add one teaspoonful of soda, half a cup of molasses, a little salt, and bake. (Comment: *half a cup of yeast?*)

# Hazelnut Biscotti

This recipe comes from a friend I've known since childhood. She now lives on a lovely ranch in Everson, Washington, but comes back East now and then to visit. Along with the recipe, she also sent hazelnuts which had grown on a tree in her back yard. M.P.

| | | | |
|---|---|---|---|
| 1 2/3 | cups hazelnuts, toasted and chopped | 2 2/3 | cups white flour |
| | | 1 | cup whole wheat flour |
| 1 1/2 | cups sugar | 6 | eggs |
| 1 | teaspoon baking powder | | dash of salt |
| 1 | teaspoon vanilla | 1 | grated orange peel |
| | melted chocolate (optional) | | |

Mix flours, sugar, baking powder, and salt. Add eggs, vanilla, and orange peel. Mix. Add hazelnuts, and knead for 5 minutes. (If very wet, knead in more flour.) Butter and flour a cookie sheet or pizza stone. Divide dough, shape into 2 logs, and place on cookie sheet. Bake 35 minutes at 350 degrees. Remove from oven. Cut logs diagonally. Place individual slices back on cookie sheets, and bake 15 minutes at 325 degrees. Cool on racks, dip tops in melted chocolate, and let biscotti cool on waxed paper. Makes lots!

*Diane Post Miller, Everson, Washington*

# Ann's Corn Muffins

This recipe and the three following it are contributed by family members, some no longer living, but still much appreciated for their love of good food and good friends.  M.P.

|   |   |
|---|---|
| 1   scant cup cornmeal | 1   scant Tablespoon flour |
| 1 1/2  teaspoons baking powder | 1 1/2  teaspoons sugar |
| 1/2  teaspoon salt | 1   egg |
| 1/2  cup milk or more | 4   Tablespoons melted lard |

Sift together cornmeal, flour, baking powder, sugar, and salt.  Beat egg.  Add milk and melted lard.  Blend 2 mixtures together.  Preheat oven to 450 degrees.  Heat greased muffin pan in oven.  Pour in batter and bake 10 minutes.

*Ann Proffitt Wine, Lynchburg, Virginia*

# Jo's Spoon Bread

This Jo, and the Ann in the title above, were sisters of Genevieve Proffitt. Bebe, as we call her, collected Jo's and Ann's recipes and later gave them to us. We are proud to have these types of family heirlooms.  M.P.

|   |   |
|---|---|
| 2   cups sweet milk | 1/2  cup corn meal |
| 1/2  teaspoon salt | 1/2  teaspoon sugar |
| 1   teaspoon baking powder | 2   eggs, separated |
| 1/2  teaspoon butter |  |

Heat milk, and add corn meal.  Cook until thick.  Remove from heat, and stir in salt, sugar, and baking powder.  Beat egg yolks; then add to mixture along with the butter.  Fold in stiffly beaten egg whites.  Bake in a greased pan at 400 degrees for 30 to 35 minutes.

*Josephine Proffitt Clements, Lynchburg, Virginia*

# Pineapple Bran Muffins

Unlike many other recipes from the same source, this one can easily fit in with today's healthy food choices. It comes from notes made in a cookbook that belonged to Jo, Ann, and Bebe's mother. The cookbook, over 100 years old, has been on our own shelf for many, many years, and it has been fun to use it in our research for this book.    M.P.

| | |
|---|---|
| 1   cup flour | 1   teaspoon soda |
| 1 1/2   teaspoon salt | 2   cups bran |
| 1 1/4   cups milk | 1/2   cup corn syrup |
| 1   cup drained, crushed pineapple | |

Mix flour, soda, and salt.  Add bran, milk, corn syrup, and pineapple.  Bake in small, greased muffin pans in 425 degree oven for about 25 minutes.

*Annie Fox Proffitt, Lynchburg, Virginia*

# Rumford Dumplings

| | |
|---|---|
| 1 1/2   cups flour | 1/2   level teaspoon salt |
| 2   level teaspoons Rumford baking powder | 2/3   cups milk |

Sift together flour, salt, and baking powder.  Add enough milk to make the mixture the consistency of biscuit dough.  Pat or roll on a board until 1/2 inch thick.  Cut into small pieces, and drop into boiling stew.  Cook 10 minutes without removing the lid of the saucepan.  If the lid is lifted before the dough is cooked, the rush of cold air may cause the dumplings to fall.  However, some people like "sad" dumplings better than fluffy ones.

*Genevieve Proffitt, Salisbury, Maryland*

# War Bread and Brown Bread

These recipes of Annie Harrell Stewart, my grandmother, were used during World War II, when sugar and eggs were scarce or not available at all, and directions for the war bread were also scarce.  M.D.

**War Bread:**

| | |
|---|---|
| 1/4 cup black molasses | 2 Tablespoons brown sugar |
| 1/4 cup cornmeal | 3/4 cup white flour |
| 1 cup graham flour | 2 teaspoons baking powder |
| 1/2 cup nuts or fruit | 1/4 cup peanuts |
| 3/4 teaspoons salt | 1 cup milk |

Put nuts into dry ingredients.  Dissolve soda in 1 tablespoon boiling water.  Put in last.  It takes about 40 minutes to bake.

**Brown Bread:**

| | |
|---|---|
| 2 cups sour milk | 1 cup molasses |
| 1 teaspoon salt | 3 1/2 cups graham flour |
| 1 1/2 cups raisins | 2 1/4 teaspoon salt |

Mix sour milk and molasses.  Stir in dry ingredients which have been sifted together.  Add floured raisins.  Mix well.  Pour into well-greased 1-pound baking powder cans and steam 6 hours.  Dry out in oven 10 minutes.

# Breakfast Gems

One cup of sweet milk, one and one-half cups of flour, one egg, one teaspoonful of salt, one teaspoonful of baking powder, beaten together five minutes. Bake in hot gem pans in a hot oven about 15 minutes.

## Old-Fashioned Spoon Bread

| | |
|---|---|
| 1 cup cornmeal | 1 teaspoon salt |
| 1 cup boiling water | 1/2 stick butter |
| 1/4 teaspoon soda | 1 cup buttermilk |
| 3 eggs, beaten separately | |

Sift meal and salt together; then pour gradually into boiling water. Mix well. Stir in butter. Stir soda into buttermilk; then pour slowly into meal mixture. Add beaten egg yolks, and mix well. Just before placing in oven, fold in stiffly beaten egg whites. Pour into a lightly greased 1 1/2-quart casserole, and bake at 375 degrees for about 50 minutes until puffed and firm to the touch.

*Sara Moss McCowen, Richmond, Virginia*


## Alene's Biscuits

Most people I know, when describing the perfect biscuit, refer to how high and light it is. Perhaps they are right, but my memories of perfect biscuits are of those that are somewhat flat, yet wonderfully flavorful. My dad made them that way, and so did our North Carolina friend Alene Fleming. I didn't have either recipe written down, so I called on Alene's daughter to send me the recipe she uses. M.P.

| | |
|---|---|
| 2 cups self-rising flour | 1/2 cup shortening |
| 1/2 cup whole milk | |

Cut shortening into flour. Add milk and stir together. Beat by hand about a minute. Put on floured paper, knead dough, and roll out. Cut into biscuits and bake at 425 degrees about 10 minutes.

*Selma Jean Everett, Hassell, North Carolina*

# Corn Dumplings

The first corn dumplings I remember eating were prepared by my sister-in-law Jeanne. She and her husband, Bud, often hosted family reunions at their cabin on the Cowpasture River, located in the mountains of Virginia near Clifton Forge. Everyone brought lots of delicious food, but we always convinced Jeanne to make corn dumplings. There are many ways to fine-tune recipes, but these directions will get you started on a luscious side dish using good, fresh corn. M.P.

3 to 4  ears fresh corn
    salt and pepper to taste
  2  cups milk, or more
    butter

4  cups water
   sugar to taste
   dumplings

Cut corn from cob, and scrape cob. Cook corn in water to which salt, pepper, and sugar have been added. Prepare your favorite dumpling recipe, or cut canned biscuits into quarters. Add milk to corn, and bring to a boil. Drop dumplings that have been coated with flour into boiling liquid. Reduce heat, cover, and cook for 10 to 12 minutes. More milk and sugar may be added, and the liquid may be thickened if desired. A big dollop of butter adds flavor.

*Jeanne Miller Proffitt, Pearisburg, Virginia*

 # Pop Overs

Four cups of flour, four eggs, four cups of milk, piece of butter the size of two nutmegs, half a teaspoonful of salt; melt the butter. (Comment: *Did all cooks instinctively know what to do just by reading these limited directions?*)

# German Dumplings

When one of our sons married into a family with German heritage, we gained a wonderful friend, our daughter-in-law's mother, Gerda. She has shared several of her recipes with me, and I happily pass them on to you. M.P.

| | |
|---|---|
| 1 to 2 eggs | 1/4 teaspoon salt |
| 1/2 eggshell of vinegar | flour |

Whip together eggs, salt, and vinegar. Add just enough flour to make a stiff batter. Drop by teaspoon into hot soup or on top of sauerkraut. Cover, and cook for 10 minutes. Remove cover; cook 15 minutes longer. For smaller dumplings, use 1/2 teaspoon. (Dip spoon in soup or kraut juice each time to prevent sticking.)

*Gerda L'Heureux, Virginia Beach, Virginia*

# Black Iron Skillet Cornbread

If you don't have a black iron skillet, get one. You may not use it much for frying, but nothing beats a well-seasoned skillet for making cornbread. M.P.

| | |
|---|---|
| 1 1/2 cups cornmeal | 2 Tablespoons baking powder |
| 1 teaspoon salt | |
| 2 eggs | 2 Tablespoon sugar |
| 1/4 cup vegetable oil | 1 1/2 cups milk |

Place iron skillet into preheated 400 degree oven for 15 minutes. While skillet is heating, mix cornmeal, baking powder, salt, and sugar. In a separate bowl, combine eggs, milk, and vegetable oil. Then blend the two mixtures. Remove skillet from oven and lightly grease immediately. Pour mixture into skillet. Bake 25 to 30 minutes or until brown.

# Mrs. Bleeker's Waffles

One quart of milk, a little sour if possible; a piece of butter the size of an egg; a piece of lard the same size; four eggs. Mix well with flour enough to make a stiff batter. If the milk is a little sour, enough soda to cover a five-cent piece will be sufficient to raise the waffles; but if it is fresh a teaspoonful of soda must be used; a teaspoonful of salt. Bake as quickly as possible.

# Cornmeal Waffles

| | |
|---|---|
| 3/4 cups sifted flour | 2 eggs, beaten separately |
| 3 teaspoons baking powder | 1 1/3 cups milk (about) |
| 1 teaspoon salt | 1 1/2 cups water ground |
| 2 Tablespoons sugar | cornmeal |
| 1/2 cup melted shortening | |

Sift together flour, baking powder, salt, and sugar. Beat eggs whites until stiff but not dry. Set aside. Beat egg yolks, and add milk. Add sifted dry ingredients to cornmeal, mixing just enough to blend. Add melted shortening. Fold in stiffly beaten egg whites. Bake in moderately hot waffle iron about 5 minutes or until done. If batter stiffens too much, add milk, a tablespoon at a time, until batter is thinned slightly. Makes 5 or 6 waffles.

*Sara Gabel, Washington, North Carolina*

# Eye-Popping Pancake

This is a recipe we sometimes use for our traditional Christmas brunch. It bakes beautifully in a black iron skillet, and the grandchildren's eyes really do pop when they peek at it through the glass window of our oven.  M.P.

| | | | |
|---|---|---|---|
| 4 | Tablespoons margarine | 4 | eggs, beaten |
| 1 | cup flour | 1 | cup milk |
| 1/2 | teaspoon salt | 2 | Tablespoons sugar |

Preheat oven to 400 degrees. Mix flour with beaten eggs. Fully blend milk and salt with egg mixture. Melt margarine in black iron skillet until it bubbles. Pour in egg mixture, and place in oven immediately. Don't even think of looking for 20 minutes!  Then sprinkle the 2 tablespoons of sugar on top of pancake, and bake another 10 minutes. Serve in wedges with syrup, hot fruit pie filling, or your favorite fresh fruit.

# Sourdough Pancakes

| | | | |
|---|---|---|---|
| 1/2 | cup sourdough starter | 2 1/2 | cups whole wheat flour |
| 2 | cups warm water | | or unbleached all-purpose |
| 3/4 | cup milk | | flour |
| 2 | Tablespoons vegetable oil | 1 | egg, beaten |
| 1 | teaspoon salt | 1 | teaspoon baking soda |
| 2 | Tablespoons brown sugar | | |

Combine starter, flour, and water; blend well. Add milk, oil, and egg; mix thoroughly. Combine salt, soda, and sugar; sprinkle over batter, and fold in gently. Let stand a few minutes. Drop batter by spoonfuls onto hot griddle, and cook until lightly browned on both sides. Fruit or nuts may be added to the batter. (To replenish starter, add 1 1/2 cups strong, bread-type flour and 1 cup warm water to unused starter. Beat until smooth; cover, and let stand in a warm place overnight. Return to refrigerator until needed.)

# Sweet Potato Biscuits

| | |
|---|---|
| 3 teaspoons baking powder | 1 cup fluffy mashed |
| 1 cup sifted flour | sweet potatoes |
| 3/4 teaspoon salt | 4 Tablespoons cold Crisco |
| 2/3 cup sweet milk or less | shortening |

Preheat oven to 450 degrees. Sift flour, salt, and baking powder together. Cut in shortening. Mix in sweet potatoes and enough milk so the dough is soft but stiff enough to handle. Put dough on floured board and mold into a ball. Do not knead. Roll to 1/2-inch thickness. Cut into rounds, and place on lightly greased and floured pan. Bake 12 to 15 minutes. Makes 8 to 10 biscuits.

# Soft Gingerbread

| | |
|---|---|
| 3 cups flour | 1/2 cup milk |
| 1/2 cup lard | 1 1/2 cups molasses |
| 1 teaspoon soda | 1 teaspoon ginger |
| 2 eggs, separated | |

Cut lard into flour. Beat egg yolks; add milk, soda, ginger, and molasses. Stir in flour mixture. Beat egg whites to a stiff froth, and fold in carefully. Bake for three quarters of an hour in a moderate oven.

# Entertaining ABC's

## Home in Washington

*Growing up in Eastern North Carolina I thought when I said I lived in Washington, everyone would know I meant the "Original Washington." The town was built along the Pamlico River, and is as lovely and friendly today as it was when I grew up in this house by the river. — M.D.*

# ENTERTAINING ABC'S

## Appetizers

When I was growing up in Washington, North Carolina, Coca Cola parties
were popular ways of entertaining during the summer months. We really didn't
need a reason or excuse to have one of these morning parties, but someone's
out-of-town company nearly always called for a get-together! Whatever the
occasion, friends were called, usually a few days in advance, by the hostess and
everyone arrived ready to enjoy each other's company, catch up on local news,
and enjoy the refreshments. Miniature sandwiches, filled pastry shells, nuts,
mints, brownies or cake, and other assorted goodies were served along with
colas or iced tea. Depending on the occasion, good china and crystal might be
used. The parties were fun and the refreshments were always delicious!
M.D.

## Cucumber Tea Sandwiches

| | |
|---|---|
| 1/2　small onion, chopped | 2　8-ounce packages cream |
| 1　large cucumber, peeled | cheese |
| and thinly sliced | 80　slices thin white bread |

Blend onion and cream cheese. Using a 2 1/2-inch biscuit cutter, cut bread
slices into rounds. Spread about 1 tablespoon cream cheese mixture on bread
rounds. Arrange cucumber slices over cream cheese mixture. Serve either
open-faced or closed, using a bread round on top.

*Mary S. Moss, Washington, North Carolina*

# Ribbon Cream Cheese and Olive Sandwiches

These sandwiches were often served at Coca Cola parties, receptions, and other occasions when light refreshments were served. The amount of ingredients would depend on the quantity of sandwiches needed. M.D.

| | |
|---|---|
| cream cheese, softened | milk |
| mayonnaise | Miracle Whip salad dressing |
| olive juice | stuffed olives, chopped |
| loaf bread | food coloring |

Combine mayonnaise, Miracle Whip, olive juice, and chopped olives with cream cheese. Add milk as needed for consistency. Blend in food coloring as desired. Spread thickly on bread. Remove crusts, and cut sandwiches into 3 or 4 rectangular strips.

*Mary S. Moss, Washington, North Carolina*

# Chili Dip

Our son Leon learned to do many household chores when he was growing up. He always liked to give parties for folks, and still does. He makes this dip when he and his wife entertain, which they often do. It can be made ahead of time and can also be frozen. M.P.

| | | | |
|---|---|---|---|
| 1 | pound lean ground beef | 1 | pound processed American cheese |
| 1 | can tomatoes and green chilies | | |
| 2 | Tablespoons Worcestershire sauce | 1/2 | teaspoon chili powder, or more |
| 1 | small onion, chopped fine | | |

Brown and drain ground beef. Add all other ingredients and stir together. Bring to boil. Cook at a fast simmer for 1 hour, stirring frequently. A crock pot may be used for the simmering process.

*Leon Proffitt, Chesapeake, Virginia*

# Smoky Meat Balls

Not only did Mary and I teach in the Virginia Beach Public School System, but our husbands did also. The four of us worked at many different locations in various capacities through the years. Along the way, we collected many recipes that we are happy to share. This one came from a teacher at Thoroughgood Elementary School. M.P.

|   |   |   |   |
|---|---|---|---|
| 2 | pounds lean ground beef | 1 | teaspoon salt |
| 1/4 | teaspoon garlic salt | 1/4 | cup chopped onion |
| 1/4 | teaspoon pepper | 1/2 | cup fine cracker crumbs |
| 1 | egg | 1 | Tablespoon salad oil |
| 1 | bottle (18 ounces) | 1/4 | cup milk |
|   | smoky-type barbecue sauce | 1 | cup water |

Mix together until lightly blended the ground beef, onion, salt, pepper, garlic salt, cracker crumbs, egg, and milk. Shape into meat balls about the size of walnuts. Brown in hot salad oil on all sides. In a large pan, mix barbecue sauce and water. Place the browned meat balls in sauce; simmer for 15 minutes. Pour meat balls and sauce into a chafing dish, and serve with small picks. Makes 8 dozen.

*Dottie McCarson, Virginia Beach, Virginia*

# Sausage Tid-Bits

|   |   |   |
|---|---|---|
| 1 | pound sausage (hot) | 3 cups Bisquick |
| 10 | ounces sharp cheese, grated | |

Mix well, like pastry. Make into small balls. Bake at 350 degrees near top of oven for about 15 to 18 minutes, on a cookie sheet. These can be frozen and reheated in 350 degree oven for about 10 minutes. Makes 100 balls the size of marbles.

*Mary S. Moss, Washington, North Carolina*

# Artichoke Dip

2   10-ounce packages frozen
    artichoke hearts
1   cup grated Parmesan cheese

1   cup mayonnaise
1   cup medium hot salsa

Thaw artichokes in microwave; chop in food processor.  In a large bowl, mix all ingredients together; pour into baking dish.  Bake at 350 degrees for approximately 20 minutes or until bubbly.

*Michelle Taylor, Virginia Beach, Virginia*

# Chicken Salad Miniatures

1   loaf thin sliced bread or
    60 miniature pastry shells
1/2   cup minced celery
1   teaspoon lemon juice
    mayonnaise

1   cup cooked chicken,
    finely chopped
1/4   cup pecans, toasted
    and chopped
    salt and pepper to taste

Combine chicken, celery, pecans, and lemon juice.  Add enough mayonnaise to moisten mixture.  Season with salt and pepper.  Fill pastry shells, or spread on bread slices that have had crusts removed.

**Pastry Shells:**
1   stick butter
1   cup flour

1   3-ounce package cream
    cheese

Mix together thoroughly.  May be put in plastic bag to mix or mix with bare hand.  Chill.  Pat or roll out, and fit into small muffin tins.  Bake about 10 minutes in 350 degree oven.

*Mary S. Moss, Washington, North Carolina*

# Cheese Biscuits

These were a Christmas tradition at our house. Mother always made these in plenty of time to have for the family and to serve to guests during the holidays. She kept the cheese biscuits in fruit cake tins. We all knew which tins had the cheese biscuits, and often we would catch each other with the lid in one hand and cheese biscuits in the other! My husband and children always start in early December asking me to make these biscuits. M.D.

| | | | |
|---|---|---|---|
| 1 | pound butter or margarine | 1 | pound sharp American |
| 1 | teaspoon cayenne pepper | | cheese, grated fine |
| 1 | small can Parmesan cheese | | pecan halves, optional |
| 4 | cups flour | | confectioners' sugar |

Cream together butter, cheeses, and pepper. Add flour and mix well. Roll out on floured board. Cut out biscuits with a 1-inch cookie cutter. Arrange on ungreased cookie sheet, and bake at 325 degrees for 10-15 minutes. If desired, a pecan half may be placed on top before baking. Let cool. Sift confectioners' sugar on top if desired. Makes about 300 cheese biscuits. Recipe can easily be cut in half.

*Mary S. Moss, Washington, North Carolina*

# Cheese Ball

| | | | |
|---|---|---|---|
| 2 | 8-ounce packages cream cheese | 1 | teaspoon onion, chopped |
| 1/4 | cup chopped green pepper | 1 | cup pecans, chopped |
| 1 | small can crushed pineapple, drained | | |

Mix and mold into ball. Refrigerate. Serve with crackers.

*Helen Taylor Clark, Wachapreague,Virginia*

# Braunschweiger Paté

| | | | |
|---|---|---|---|
| 1 | pound Braunschweiger | 1 | Tablespoon milk |
| 1 | package green onion dip mix | 1/8 | teaspoon hot pepper sauce |
| 1 | teaspoon sugar | 1/8 | teaspoon garlic powder |
| 1 | 8-ounce package cream cheese | | |

Bring liverwurst and cream cheese to room temperature.  Mash liverwurst, and mix with dip mix, garlic powder, sugar, and 2 ounces of cream cheese.  Form into one igloo shape or 2 loaves and chill.  Mix milk and 6 ounces of cream cheese.  Spread over mold and chill.  Serve with rye crackers, Melba toast, Ritz crackers, or small rounds from party-size pumpernickel bread.

*Bayside Junior High  School, Virginia Beach, Virginia*

# Crab Swiss Bites

| | | | |
|---|---|---|---|
| 1 | can lump crabmeat | 4 | ounces Swiss cheese |
| 1 | spring onion, diced with stem | 1/2 | cup mayonnaise |
| 1/4 | teaspoon curry | 1/2 | teaspoon lemon juice |
| 1 | package butterflake rolls | 1 | small can water chestnuts, sliced |

Combine crabmeat, cheese, onion, mayonnaise, curry, lemon juice.  Separate sections of rolls.  Top with 1 slice water chestnut and 1 teaspoon of crab mixture.  Bake on ungreased sheet for 10 minutes at 400 degrees.

*Rose Snyder, Jensen Beach, Florida*

# Salmon Ball

1   15 1/2-ounce can red salmon
1   Tablespoon minced onion
1   Tablespoon lemon juice
1/2  teaspoon liquid smoke

1   8-ounce package Neufchâtel
    cheese, softened
1   teaspoon horseradish

Drain and flake salmon.  Combine with all other ingredients. Shape into ball.
Chill 2 hours, or until firm.  Serve with crackers.

*Margaret Taylor Proffitt, Virginia Beach, Virginia*

# Sesame Dip

1/4  teaspoon ginger
2   teaspoons soy sauce
1/3  cup toasted sesame seeds

1/4  teaspoon curry powder
1/2  cup real mayonnaise
1   8-ounce container sour cream

Combine ginger, curry, and soy sauce.  Gradually stir in mayonnaise and sour
cream. Stir in toasted sesame seeds.  (To toast sesame seeds, spread in pie pan,
bake in a preheated 350 degree oven, about 10 minutes or until a light golden
brown, stirring frequently.)  Makes 2 cups.

# Shrimp Spread

2   cans shrimp
    dash of garlic salt
2   green onions, finely chopped
    mayonnaise

    dash of lemon juice
2   stalks of celery, finely
    chopped

Rinse and mash shrimp.  Add finely chopped celery, onion, and other ingredients.  Mix in enough mayonnaise to bind together.

# Beverages

 ## Fruit Punch

Juice of 10 lemons
Juice of 10 oranges and some grapefruit juice
As much water as you want, and put in a bottle of grape juice to color it
To make it better mash a pineapple and some bananas.
Combine all ingredients for a delicious punch!

*Annie Harrell Stewart, Charlotte, North Carolina*

 ## Punch

| | |
|---|---|
| Any good tea — cooled | 1 quart grape juice |
| 25-cent can of grated pineapple | 1/2 dozen lemons |
| ginger ale (about 1 bottle) or | |
| ginger extract, as you like. | |

Add any other fruits, cherries, oranges, etc. Sweeten to taste and serve ice cold. Use more than half of tea and use as much of the other ingredients as you want and need.

*Annie Harrell Stewart, Charlotte, North Carolina*

# Iced Coffee Punch

Mother served this for a D.A.R. meeting on September 17, 1958, along with chicken salad sandwiches, cheese biscuits, nuts, mints, and decorated cake squares. M.D.

| | |
|---|---|
| 1 gallon double strength instant coffee, cooled | 1 gallon vanilla ice cream |
| | 1 1/2 pints whipping cream |

Add ice cream to cold coffee. Stir. Fold in whipped cream. Chill by adding regular strength coffee ice cubes.

*Mary S. Moss, Washington, North Carolina*

# Carpenters' Punch

| | |
|---|---|
| 2 46-ounce cans berry Hawaiian fruit punch, chilled | 1 12-ounce can lemonade concentrate, thawed |
| 2 24-ounce bottles white grape juice, chilled | |

Combine all ingredients. Serve over ice. Makes about 20 cups.

# Champagne Punch

| | |
|---|---|
| 1 1/2 cups sugar | 2 cups lemon juice |
| 2 fifths Sauterne, chilled | 1 fifth champagne, chilled |
| 1/2 cup Cointreau (optional) | 1/2 cup brandy (optional) |
| 1 lemon, sliced | 1 1/2 cups strawberries, sliced |

Combine sugar and lemon juice. Stir until sugar is dissolved. Chill thoroughly. Just before serving, pour over ice in punch bowl. Stir in Sauterne and champagne. Add Cointreau and brandy, if desired. Garnish with lemon slices and strawberries.

# English Wassail

Ladled from a plain old crock or a fancy silver bowl, the combined ingredients of this recipe provide a wonderful aroma that only adds to the holiday festivities of Christmastime. It also provides an opportunity to explain to the little ones that a wassail is a drink used for especially festive occasions. Grandma, in order to further explain, might sing a quick chorus of "Here we Come A-Wassailing." This usually sends the grandchildren quickly on their way. You will probably like this flavorful quaff, but my advice to all you grandmas: Don't sing! M.P.

| | |
|---|---|
| 1 quart apple cider | 1 cup orange juice |
| 1/2 teaspoon honey | 1/3 cup lemon juice |
| 1 stick cinnamon | |

In 2 quart sauce pan, warm cider over low heat. Add other ingredients and let simmer for 8 to 10 minutes. Serve while still warm.

# Daiquiri Punch

| | |
|---|---|
| 2 6-ounce cans frozen limeade, thawed | 1 6-ounce can frozen lemonade, thawed |
| 1 6-ounce can frozen orange juice, thawed | 1 fifth rum |
| 8 cups water, chilled | 4 cups carbonated water, chilled |

Combine fruit juices with 8 cups of water and chill. Combine mixture, 4 cups of carbonated water, and rum in punch bowl. Delicious but potent! Use less rum if desired.

# Conversation Snacks

## Crêpes Beignets with Raspberry Dip

18  baked crêpes (7 inches)             vegetable oil for frying
    cinnamon-sugar or powdered
    sugar

Make 3 stacks of 6 crêpes each.  Cut each stack with a sharp knife into 1-inch strips.  Separate.  Pour oil into sauce pan or deep fat fryer to a depth of 1 1/2 inches.  Heat oil to moderate 350 degrees.  Drop a handful of strips into hot oil.  Fry until golden and crisp, about 1 minute, poking strips down constantly with slotted spoon.  Drain strips on paper towels.  Dust with cinnamon-sugar or powdered sugar.  Serve beignets warm or cold with hot dip.  Makes about 10 servings (a dozen beignets each).

**Brandied Raspberry Dip:**
1  12-ounce jar raspberry          1/4  cup brandy
   preserves                         1  teaspoon lemon juice

Stir ingredients together, and heat to just below boiling.  Serve hot with beignets.  Makes 1 1/3 cups.

 ## Shelling Nuts

If you soak nuts in salt water overnight and then crack them by striking on the end, the meats will come out whole.

# Sally Lunn Muffins

| | | | |
|---|---|---|---|
| 1 1/2 | sticks butter | 2/3 | cup sugar |
| 3 | eggs | 3 | cups self-rising flour |
| 1 | cup milk | | |

Cream butter and sugar together. Add eggs and mix. To these ingredients, alternately stir in flour and milk. Bake at 400 degrees in greased muffin tins. Small muffins cook 5 minutes; larger muffins take longer. These freeze well.

*Mary S. Moss, Washington, North Carolina*

# Sticky Buns

| | | | |
|---|---|---|---|
| 1 | package frozen bread rolls | 1/2 | cup walnuts or more |
| 1/2 | cup raisins or more (optional) | 1 | teaspoon cinnamon |
| 1 | stick butter, melted | 1 | small vanilla pudding |
| 1/2 | cup brown sugar | | (not instant) |

Place nuts and raisins in bottom of a greased bundt pan. Arrange rolls on top. Mix together dry pudding, brown sugar, and cinnamon. Put over rolls. Pour melted butter over all of the above. Cover with greased wax paper and a wet dish towel. Let rise on countertop overnight (about 10 hours). Bake at 350 degrees for 25 to 30 minutes. Cool 10 minutes and invert on plate.

# Salted Pecans

| | | | |
|---|---|---|---|
| 1 | pound shelled pecan halves | 2 | Tablespoons margarine |
| | salt | | |

Melt margarine; then stir into shelled pecan halves. Sprinkle with salt. Spread nuts on cookie sheet. Bake in oven on low heat until crisp.

*June Hand-Decker, Virginia Beach, Virginia*

# Petite Cherry Tarts

| | |
|---|---|
| 2 large packages cream cheese | 2 eggs |
| 1/2 cup sugar | 1 Tablespoon lemon juice |
| 1 teaspoon vanilla | vanilla wafers |
| 1 can cherry pie filling | |

Mix cream cheese, eggs, sugar, lemon juice, and vanilla with fork until blended; then beat with electric mixer. Put muffin papers in muffin tins. Place a vanilla wafer in bottom of each paper, and fill half full with cream cheese mixture. Bake for 15 minutes at 350 degrees. Add cherry pie filling to top of muffins. Chill in refrigerator. Makes 2 dozen small tarts.

*Mary S. Moss, Washington, North Carolina*

# Pecan Tarts

**Crust:**

| | |
|---|---|
| 1 3-ounce package cream cheese | 1/2 cup butter |
| | 1 cup flour |
| dash of salt | |

Mix well. Form into balls and press into small muffin tins.

**Filling:**

| | |
|---|---|
| 3/4 cup brown sugar | 1 egg |
| 1 Tablespoon butter | 1 teaspoon vanilla |
| chopped pecans | |

Beat egg. Add other ingredients. Spoon into tins. Bake 35 to 40 minutes at 350 degrees. Makes 24 tarts.

# Kentucky Bourbon Balls

| | | | |
|---|---|---|---|
| 1 | large box glazed cherries | 1 | pint Kentucky bourbon |
| 1 | box semi-sweet chocolate | 1/4 | pound butter or margarine |
| 2 | pounds powdered sugar | | pinch of salt |
| 3/4 | bar of paraffin, melted | | plastic toothpick |

Cut glazed cherries in half, and marinate in bourbon overnight or longer. In a large bowl, cut 1/4 pound of butter or margarine into 2 pounds of powdered sugar. Add a pinch of salt and enough bourbon to make dough workable (about 13 tablespoons). Drain marinated cherries. Pinch off small amount of dough and flatten between fingers. Place half a cherry in middle of dough, fold over and around, then shape into small ball and place on waxed paper that has been put over bottom of cookie sheet. Refrigerate overnight. The next day, dip each ball in bourbon. Place back on cookie sheet, and refrigerate again overnight.

**Chocolate coating:**
Melt box of semi-sweet chocolate in top of double boiler. Melt paraffin, add to chocolate, and mix well. Turn off heat. Stab ball with toothpick; dip into chocolate. Let excess chocolate drip back into pan. Drop ball back onto waxed paper. When all balls have been coated, fill in holes left by stick. Refrigerate. When chocolate has set, balls may be transferred to another container for continued storage in refrigerator.

# Main Dishes

## Coast Guard Station

*Several of my ancestors were mariners. They must
surely have been grateful for the life saving services
provided to seamen along the Virginia and
North Carolina coasts — M.P.*

# MAIN DISHES
## Beef

## Ann's Meat Loaf

| | | | |
|---|---|---|---|
| 1 1/2 | pounds round steak, ground | 1 1/2 | pounds pork, ground |
| 3 | eggs, slightly beaten | 1 | cup cracker crumbs |
| 4 | teaspoons salt | 8 | Tablespoons sweet milk |
| 3 | teaspoons sage | 1 | teaspoon pepper |
| | flour | | Butter the size of an egg |

Mix ground steak and pork together. Add all other ingredients and mix well. Form into loaf, dust rather heavily with flour, and place in pan. Add a little water, and cover for baking. Bake in 350 to 400 degree oven for about 2 hours. Serves 6.

*Ann Proffitt Wine, Lynchburg, Virginia*

 ## Meat Loaf

This recipe appears exactly as I found it among my grandmother's recipes. No directions and no explanation of scraps! M.D.

| | | | |
|---|---|---|---|
| 25 | cents worth scraps | 5 | cents worth frankfurters, weeny, or ham |
| 1 | Tablespoon onion, cooked | | |
| 1 | Tablespoon of green peppers | 1/2 | cup thick brown sauce, or |
| 1 | cup bread crumbs, crushed | 1 | whole egg |

# Meat Loaf

| | | | |
|---|---|---|---|
| 2 | pounds ground beef | | handful corn flakes or bran flakes |
| 3 | Tablespoons Worcestershire sauce | 1 | slice bacon, minced |
| | onion juice | | black pepper |
| | Adolph salt | 1 | egg, unbeaten |
| 2 | slices bacon (reserve) | | |

Mix well. Shape into loaf. Place the 2 strips of bacon in bottom of pan. Place meat loaf on top. Bake in aluminum foil-lined biscuit pan at 350 degrees for 1 hour.

*Mary S. Moss, Washington, North Carolina*

# Hamburger Quiche

My friend Ruth gave me this recipe several years ago. It is a really special way to fix ground beef. Add a salad and fruit or vegetable for a quick and easy — and good dinner. M.D.

| | | | |
|---|---|---|---|
| 1 | unbaked pie shell | 1/2 | pound ground beef |
| 1/2 | cup mayonnaise | 1/2 | cup milk |
| 2 | eggs | 1 | Tablespoon cornstarch |
| 1/3 | cup sliced onion | 1 1/2 | cups sharp Cheddar cheese, chopped |
| | mushrooms (optional) | | |

Brown beef and drain off fat. Mix mayonnaise, milk, eggs, and cornstarch. Stir in beef, cheese, and onion. Turn into pastry shell. Bake 35 to 40 minutes at 350 degrees or until brown on top and knife comes out clean.

*Ruth Barco, Virginia Beach, Virginia*

# Spaghetti Casserole

| | | | |
|---|---|---|---|
| 3 | Tablespoons bacon drippings | | onion |
| | green pepper | 1 | pound hamburger |
| 1 | can tomatoes | 1 | can tomato sauce |
| | salt and pepper | 1 | can mushrooms |
| | oregano | | spaghetti, cooked |
| 1/2 | pound Cheddar cheese, cubed | | |

Simmer onion and green pepper in bacon drippings. Add hamburger, tomatoes, tomato sauce, seasonings, and mushrooms. Sprinkle oregano on top and cook 15 minutes. Pour over cooked spaghetti. Mix and pour into baking dish. Spread cubed cheese on top. Bake 30 minutes in 350 degree oven. May be prepared the day before and baked later.

*Mary S. Moss, Washington, North Carolina*

# Spaghetti

| | | | |
|---|---|---|---|
| 2 | Tablespoons bacon drippings | 1 | minced onion |
| 1 | pound ground beef | 1 | can tomatoes |
| 1/4 | green pepper, minced | 2 | Tablespoons celery, |
| | salt | | minced |
| | cayenne pepper | | spaghetti |

Brown minced onion in bacon drippings. Remove onions and set aside. Slowly brown ground beef, and return onion to pan. Add tomatoes, green pepper, celery, and seasonings. Cover and let cook for 45 minutes on medium heat. Serve with cooked spaghetti.

*Mary S. Moss, Washington, North Carolina*

# Spaghetti Sauce

My remarkable daughter-in-law Jennifer, in spite of her own busy life, always finds time to help others. Mary and I can never thank her enough for the wonderful illustrations she has contributed to this book. M.P.

| | |
|---|---|
| 1 jar prepared spaghetti sauce | 2 14-ounce cans tomatoes |
| 1 10-ounce can tomato paste | 1 cup water |
| 1 green pepper, chopped | 1 small onion, chopped |
| 1 teaspoon oregano | 1 8-ounce package sliced |
| 3 bay leaves | pepperoni |
| salt to taste | 1/4 teaspoon dried red peppers |

Combine all ingredients in pot; simmer for 2 hours. Use with spaghetti or any other favorite pasta.

*Jennifer Taylor Proffitt, Virginia Beach, Virginia*

# Beef Roast

| | |
|---|---|
| 1 3- to 4-pound lean beef roast | 1 8-ounce can tomato sauce |
| 1 teaspoon prepared mustard | 1 teaspoon brown sugar |
| 1 teaspoon prepared horseradish | 1 slice of bacon, cooked and |
| 3 carrots, cut in large pieces | crumbled |
| 4 onions, quartered | 4 potatoes, halved |

Place beef roast in baking dish. Combine tomato sauce, mustard, brown sugar, horseradish, and bacon. Spread over roast. Cover with foil; bake in 325 degree oven for 2 hours. Remove from oven; add carrots, onions, and potatoes. Re-cover, and return to oven. Bake another hour, or until vegetables are done.

*Margaret Taylor Proffitt, Virginia Beach, Virginia*

# Pot Roast

When Mother gave me this recipe several years ago, she told me the roast was worth every minute of the time it took to prepare it. I agree! It is delicious! M.D.

| | | | |
|---|---|---|---|
| 1 | 2 1/2- to 3-pound roast | 1/3 | cup red wine (Burgundy) |
| 1/2 | cup green pepper, chopped | 1/2 | cup onion chopped |
| 1 | clove garlic, minced, | 2 1/2 | teaspoons salt |
| | or garlic salt | 2 | Tablespoons shortening, or |
| 1 1/4 | teaspoons pepper | | oil |
| 1 | can tomato sauce | | |

Combine all ingredients except meat, tomato sauce, and shortening. Pour over meat as a marinade. Marinate at least 2 hours or overnight. Turn several times. Drain meat; save marinade. Brown roast in shortening. Add tomato sauce and marinade. Cover. Simmer 2 1/2 hours.

*Mary S. Moss, Washington, North Carolina*

# Eye of Round Roast

| | | |
|---|---|---|
| 1 | 5-pound eye of round roast, | salt |
| | or larger | pepper |

Put in 350 degree oven, uncovered. Use a shallow roasting pan without a rack. Do not add water. Bake about 30 minutes per pound. Baste frequently while the roast is cooking. During last half hour, add a little water. After removing from oven, cover with foil. Cut very thin slices while it is still slightly warm. Delicious served cold with horseradish-mustard sauce. Good for buffet when served with party rye bread, or pumpernickel.

*Mary S. Moss, Washington, North Carolina*

# Rouladen

This delicious beef dish was prepared for us by our daughter-in-law Susan at our first meal with her and our son Michael after they were married. Susan inherited her mother's cooking talent, and Michael inherited his father's love for baking. Together they presented a wonderful dinner. M.P.

breakfast steak, 6 to 8 slices
chopped onion
salt and pepper to taste
brown gravy

bacon, 6 to 8 slices,
uncooked
mustard

Tenderize steaks. Salt and pepper to taste. Spread a generous amount of mustard on each steak. Put one slice of uncooked bacon on each steak. Sprinkle with chopped onion, roll up steak, and secure with a toothpick. Brown in skillet, and simmer 45 minutes to an hour in your favorite brown gravy or, as a perfect complement to your rouladen, use a German bratten sauce (a brown gravy mixture) which can be purchased in the Virginia Beach area at The German Pantry.

*Susan Proffitt, Virginia Beach, Virginia*

 **Meat Tenderizer**

Lay meat a few minutes in a strong vinegar water. (Never allow fresh meat to remain in paper, it absorbs the juices.)

# Easy Chili

| | |
|---|---|
| 1 pound lean ground beef | 1 teaspoon chili powder |
| 1 small onion, chopped | salt and pepper to taste |
| 1 can chili beans | 1 can kidney beans |
| 1 32-ounce can tomato juice | |

Brown meat and onions. Drain. Add remaining ingredients. Cover and simmer over low heat for 2 to 3 hours.

# Pepper Steak with Cheddar Noodles

| | |
|---|---|
| 1/4 cup butter (1/2 stick) | 1 1/2 pounds beef (round or sirloin tip), cut in strips |
| 1/8 teaspoon garlic powder | |
| 1/3 cup chopped onion | 1 1/2 green peppers, julienned |
| 1 1-pound can tomatoes | 1 beef boullion cube |
| 1 Tablespoon cornstarch | 2 Tablespoons water |
| 2 Tablespoons soy sauce | 1 teaspoon sugar |
| 1/2 teaspoon salt | 3 cups wide noodles |
| 1 cup shredded Cheddar cheese | |

In a 10-inch skillet, melt butter. Add beef and sprinkle with garlic powder. Sauté, stirring occasionally until browned. Remove meat from skillet. Add onion and green pepper; sauté two minutes. Return meat to skillet with tomatoes and boullion cube. If using round steak, simmer 15 to 20 minutes. If using sirloin tip, simmer 5 minutes. Blend together corn starch, water, soy sauce, sugar, and salt. Add to meat mixture and cook, stirring constantly until thickened. Reduce heat and cook 2 additional minutes. Meanwhile, prepare noodles according to package directions. Drain and toss with Cheddar cheese. To serve, spoon pepper steak over Cheddar noodles.

*Emily Groover Shelley, Virginia Beach, Virginia*

# Pork

## Baked Country Ham

There is a story about a young woman who had cut off the end of the ham she was cooking. When asked why she had cut the end off the ham, she replied, "I don't know, my mother always cut off one end of her hams." She asked her mother why she did it. Her mother replied, "It was because the ham wouldn't fit in the pot." I learned much of what I know about cooking from watching my mother. However, she usually explained the hows and whys! M.D.

Notice the weight of the ham. Wash ham. Soak in water to cover several hours, depending on how salty you want the ham to be. The bone may be removed before ham is cooked if desired. Wrap in heavy aluminum foil. Put on rack in a roaster. Add 4 cups water and put the lid on. Preheat oven to 500 degrees. Put ham in the oven. (Careful: Don't burn your hand.) Cook 1 minute per pound. Turn oven off. Wait 3 hours. Turn oven back on to 500 degrees. When oven reaches that heat, cook ham 1 minute per pound again. Cut oven off and leave ham in oven overnight. Do NOT open the oven door ANY TIME after you first put the ham in the oven until you remove it the next morning.

*Mary S. Moss, Washington, North Carolina*

## Pork Chop Casserole

| | | | |
|---|---|---|---|
| 4 to 5 | large potatoes, sliced | 2 | large onions, sliced |
| 1/2 | can mushroom soup | 6 to 8 | pork chops |

In a buttered casserole, layer sliced potatoes, sliced onions and mushroom soup. Brown pork chops; place on top. Bake at 350 degrees for 1 hour.

# Pork Chop With Amber Rice

| | | | |
|---|---|---|---|
| 6 | pork chops, 3/4 inch thick | 1 1/3 | cups instant rice |
| 1 | cup orange juice | 1 | can chicken-rice soup |
| | salt and pepper | | |

Brown pork chops in skillet. Season with salt and pepper. Spread rice in bottom of a 12x10x2-inch baking dish. Carefully pour orange juice over rice. Arrange browned pork chops on rice. Pour soup over all. Cover and bake in a 350 degree oven for 45 minutes. Uncover and bake an additional 10 minutes.

# Beans with Ham Hock

I know! I know! Ham hocks are loaded with fat, but I must include this recipe. I've often heard my husband reminisce about the family dinners at his home in Clifton Forge, Virginia, during The Depression days . His mother would prepare a huge pot of delicious beans (flavored with ham hocks) and serve them along with her equally delicious hot rolls (made with lard). No one in the family complained then and probably wouldn't now. I'm sure many other households in those days were glad to have moms who could provide such good tasting food during such bad economic times. M.P.

| | | | |
|---|---|---|---|
| 6 | cups water | 1 | medium onion, chopped |
| 2 | small bay leaves | 1/4 | teaspoon garlic powder |
| 1 | Tablespoon parsley flakes | 1/8 | teaspoon cayenne pepper |
| 1/2 | teaspoon coarse ground black pepper | 1 | Tablespoon Old Bay seasoning |
| 2 | teaspoons salt | 1 | smoked ham hock |
| | | 1 | pound beans, your choice |

Pick through beans, and rinse. Add beans to water, and bring to a boil; boil 2 minutes. Reduce heat to a simmer. Add all other ingredients. Simmer for 2 hours or until beans are tender.

*Don Proffitt, Virginia Beach, Virginia*

# Lasagna

The Proffitts and the DeFilippos have been friends for years. We are more like family, really, and have truly experienced much of life together, both happiness and, at times, sorrow. However, we always seem to find a way to enjoy a good meal. It's what we do best. This lasagna was almost the end of Don and Jack once when they polished off almost a full pan of the following recipe at one sitting. M.P.

| | | | |
|---|---|---|---|
| 1 | pound Italian pork sausage or ground beef | 1 | clove garlic, minced |
| 1 | Tablespoon basil | 1 | Tablespoon chopped parsley |
| 1 | 1-pound can tomatoes | 1 1/2 | teaspoons salt |
| 1 | 10-ounce package of lasagna, or wide noodles | 2 | 6-ounce cans tomato paste |
| 2 | eggs, beaten | 1 | 12-ounce carton large curd, cream-style cottage cheese |
| 1/2 | teaspoon pepper | 2 | teaspoons salt |
| 1/2 | cup grated Parmesan cheese | 2 | Tablespoons chopped parsley |
| | | 1 | pound mozzarella cheese, sliced thin |

Brown meat slowly; spoon off fat. Add garlic, parsley, basil, 1 1/2 teaspoons salt, tomatoes, and tomato paste to meat. Simmer, uncovered, until thick (45 minutes to 1 hour), stirring occasionally. Cook noodles until tender. Drain and rinse in cold water. Combine cottage cheese with beaten eggs, 2 teaspoons of salt, pepper, parsley, and Parmesan cheese. Place half of the noodles in a 13x9x2-inch baking dish. Spread half of the cottage cheese mixture over the noodles. Next, spread on half of the mozzarella cheese and half of the meat mixture. Repeat layers. Bake in 375 degree oven for 30 minutes. Let stand 10 to 15 minutes before cutting.

*Joann DeFilippo, Virginia Beach, Virginia*

# Ham and Noodle Casserole

| | | | |
|---|---|---|---|
| 3/4 | cup diced onions | 1/2 | cup diced green pepper |
| 2 | teaspoons salad oil | 1 | 6-ounce package noodles |
| 1 | can whole tomatoes | 1 | cup water |
| 1 1/2 | cups diced ham | 1 | teaspoon salt |
| 1/4 | teaspoon pepper | 1/2 | teaspoon paprika |
| 1/2 | pound Cheddar cheese, chopped | | buttered bread crumbs |

Cook onions and green pepper slowly in oil until transparent but not brown. Add uncooked noodles, tomatoes, water, ham, salt, pepper, and paprika. Simmer 10 minutes. Stir in cheese. Turn into a greased 2-quart casserole, and top with bread crumbs. Bake in 350 degree oven for 40 to 45 minutes.

# Quiche Lorraine

| | | | |
|---|---|---|---|
| 1 | 9-inch unbaked pie shell | 3/4 | cup grated Swiss cheese |
| 7 | slices bacon, fried crisp, and crumbled | 3 | eggs |
| | | 1 1/2 | cups milk |
| | pinch of sugar | | pinch of nutmeg |
| | pinch cayenne pepper | | pinch of black pepper |

Bake pie shell at 400 degrees for ten minutes. Remove from oven, and turn temperature back to 300 degrees. Sprinkle cooked, crumbled bacon over bottom of pie shell. Spread grated cheese over bacon. Beat together eggs and milk; add sugar, nutmeg, cayenne pepper and black pepper. Carefully pour egg mixture into crust and bake at 300 degrees for 35 to 40 minutes.

# Barbecued Hot Dogs

Lawrence Proffitt, my father-in-law, was one of the most fun-loving people I have ever known. He loved his family and made each of us who married into it feel as if we had always belonged there. This recipe was his specialty. I still have the original copy that he typed up for me on his ancient typewriter. It has long since become stained with Worcestershire sauce and other seasonings, as it was often used when our sons were young. It was one of their favorites and still is. M.P.

| | |
|---|---|
| 2 Tablespoons butter or margarine | 1/4 cup onion, finely chopped |
| 2 Tablespoons brown sugar | 2 Tablespoons pure cider vinegar |
| 3/4 cup tomato catsup | 1 Tablespoon Worcestershire sauce |
| 1 Tablespoon prepared mustard | |
| 3/4 cup water | 1/2 teaspoon salt |
| 1/2 cup chopped celery | 1 pound hot dogs |

Cook onions in butter until brown. Add rest of ingredients except hot dogs. Cook over moderate heat for 20 minutes or until thickened. Place hot dogs in sauce. Cover with lid and cook slowly for 20 to 30 minutes. Serve hot, on buns if desired. Most delicious.

*Lawrence Proffitt, Roanoke, Virginia*

# Ham and Sweet Potato Casserole

| | | | |
|---|---|---|---|
| 1 1/2 | pounds cooked ham | 3 | pounds sweet potatoes, cooked |
| 1 | 8 1/4-ounce can sliced pineapple, drained | 1/2 | cup chopped pecans |
| 3/4 | cup maple syrup | | |

Cut ham into slices.  Peel and thickly slice potatoes.  Arrange alternate slices of potatoes and ham in a 9-inch pie pan or 2-quart shallow casserole.  Cut sliced pineapple into halves; tuck into casserole.  Sprinkle nuts over surface.  Bake in preheated 350 degree oven for 15 minutes.  Pour syrup over all.  Continue to bake 15 to 20 minutes more or until hot and bubbly.  Makes 6 servings.

# Breakfast Favorite

Most families, whether on purpose or by habit, observe certain practices at special holiday times.  Our Christmas celebration begins with my husband and me preparing brunch for our three sons, their wives, and our grandchildren.  This egg recipe can include any number of additional or varying ingredients, but I think there would be rebellion in our family if dad prepared it any way other than presented here.  M.P.

| | | | |
|---|---|---|---|
| 4 | slices bread, cubed | 1 | cup sharp cheese, grated |
| 1 | pound sausage | 8 | eggs |
| 2 | cups milk | 1 | teaspoon salt |
| 1 | teaspoon dry mustard | | |

In a greased 9x13-inch baking dish, arrange layers of bread cubes, cooked and crumbled sausage, and cheese.  Beat together eggs, salt, mustard, and milk.  Pour egg mixture over bread cubes.  Cover and refrigerate overnight.  Bake, uncovered, in a 350 degree oven for 45 minutes.  Serves 8 to 10.

*Don Proffitt, Virginia Beach, Virginia*

# Poultry

# Coq au Vin

This recipe brings back memories of a wonderful visit to France many years ago when my aunt and uncle were living in Orléans. M.D.

| | | | |
|---|---|---|---|
| 1 | cup water | 4 | or 5 chicken livers |
| 8 | chicken thighs, skin removed | 3 | Tablespoons butter |
| 2 | slices or 1/2 cup lean salt pork or bacon | 1 | Tablespoon flour |
| | | 12 | small yellow onions |
| 1 | cup chicken broth (2 boullion cubes in a cup of hot water) | 1 | cup of good Burgundy wine |
| | | 1 | teaspoon thyme |
| 2 | laurel leaves | | |

This recipe will taste better if prepared the day before it is to be served. In a small saucepan, bring a cup of water to boil with the chicken livers. Cook 2 minutes. Remove from heat and set aside. In a large sauce pan, melt 2 tablespoons of butter over medium heat. Sauté the small pork pieces, the onions (whole), and the chicken. While the chicken is cooking, start the wine sauce. In a small pan, melt 1 tablespoon of butter. Add 1 tablespoon of flour, stir well. Slowly add the wine (at room temperature), and the warm chicken broth. Slowly bring to a boil; then reduce heat. With a fork, mash the liver in a purée and add it to the wine sauce. Add thyme and laurel. Pour sauce over chicken. Cover and simmer for 1 hour.

*Jeannine Moss, Winston-Salem, North Carolina*

# Baked Chicken with Sour Cream

| | | | |
|---|---|---|---|
| 4 | chicken breasts, halved | 1 | cup sour cream |
| 1 | 3-ounce can mushrooms | 1/3 | cup slivered almonds |
| 1/3 | cup sherry | 1 | can cream of mushroom |
| | salt, pepper, paprika | | soup |

Except for the chicken breasts, combine all other ingredients. Pour over the chicken breasts, and bake uncovered in 350 degree oven for 1 hour. After 1 hour, turn heat lower and cover. Cook 1 hour longer.

# Chicken Divan

| | | | |
|---|---|---|---|
| 6 | whole chicken breasts, cooked | 3 | packages frozen broccoli |
| | | 1 | can celery soup |
| 1/4 | cup milk | 1/4 | teaspoon nutmeg |
| 1/2 | cup mayonnaise | 1/2 | cup heavy cream |
| 3 | Tablespoons sherry | 1 | teaspoon Worcestershire |
| 1/2 | can cream of chicken soup | | sauce |
| 3/4 | cup Parmesan cheese | 1/2 | cup slivered almonds |

Cook broccoli and drain well. Heat celery soup, milk, nutmeg, mayonnaise, cream, sherry, Worcestershire sauce, and cream of chicken soup. Cut each cooked chicken breast into 4 pieces. Place cooked broccoli in baking dish. Arrange chicken on top of broccoli. Pour sauce over all. Sprinkle Parmesan cheese and toasted almond slivers on top. Heat thoroughly in 350 degree oven. Serves 12.

*Mary S. Moss, Washington, North Carolina*

# Chicken à la Nell

8 boneless chicken breasts    water
  salt, pepper    1 can cream of celery soup
1 jar chopped pimentos    butter or margarine
  bacon bits    paprika

Put breasts, inside up, in a baking dish. Add enough water to cover bottom of pan. Sprinkle with salt and pepper, and spoon celery soup on top. Spread chopped pimentos over chicken, and dot with butter or margarine. Seal with foil. Bake for 1 hour in a 375 degree oven. Uncover and baste. Sprinkle paprika on top, bake another 1/2 hour, and baste again. Sprinkle bacon bits on top. Cover again to keep hot.

*Mary S. Moss, Washington, North Carolina*

# Marinated Chicken Breasts

4 boneless chicken breasts,    1 16-ounce bottle French
  halved     dressing
2 cans whole cranberry sauce    1 package onion soup mix

Combine last 3 ingredients. Place chicken breasts in baking dish. Spread cranberry mixture over chicken, and marinate for 4 or more hours before baking in a 400 degree oven for 1 to 1 1/4 hours. Serve over cooked noodles. (An alternate marinade may be made from 1 jar of apricot jam and 1 bottle of Russian dressing.)

*Eleanor Cooke, Virginia Beach, Virginia*

# Chicken Pot Pie

| | | | |
|---|---|---|---|
| 1 | whole chicken | 1 | onion, chopped |
| 2 | chicken boullion cubes | 4 | Tablespoons margarine |
| 3 or 4 | Tablespoons flour | 1/2 | cup milk |
| 1 to 3 | cups chicken broth | | pastry |

Boil whole chicken in water to which onion and chicken boullion cubes have been added. Bone chicken, and leave in broth to keep warm. Melt margarine in heavy skillet. Add 3 or 4 tablespoons of flour to make smooth mixture. Stir in milk. Add chicken broth to mixture, a little at a time. Cook over low heat until smooth and a little thick. Add more broth if needed. Remove from heat. Prepare pastry mix (Martha White's Biscuit Mix, or similar). Divide into two parts. Roll out one to fit deep pie dish. Fill dish with chicken. Cover completely with gravy mixture, and top with other half of pastry. Bake 15 to 25 minutes in 350 degree oven until top is done.

# Chicken or Turkey Casserole

| | | | |
|---|---|---|---|
| 2 | cups raw spaghetti | 1/4 | cup chopped green pepper |
| 1/2 | medium onion, chopped | 2 | cups grated sharp cheese |
| 1 | teaspoon salt | 1/4 | cup sliced pimento |
| 2 | cups chicken or turkey | 1 | can mushroom soup, |
| 1/4 | cup chicken broth | | undiluted |

Break spaghetti into 2-inch lengths. Cook and drain well. Reserving 1/4 cup grated cheese, add green pepper, onion, cheese, salt, and pimento to spaghetti. Cut chicken or turkey into 2-inch pieces, and along with mushroom soup and chicken broth, add to spaghetti mixture. Pour into baking pan, and sprinkle 1/4 cup of cheese on top. Bake at 325 degrees until thoroughly heated. Can be made the day before and put in refrigerator.

# Easy Chicken "Pie"

Jean Ann is our fifth generation Proffitt cook. Her mother "Corky" and her grandmother Jeanne, her great-grandmother Mae, as well as her great-great-grandmother Annie, have also shared recipes with us for this book. M.P.

| | |
|---|---|
| 4  boneless chicken breasts | 1  can cream of celery soup |
| 1  can cream of chicken soup | 1  can chicken broth reserved |
| 1  can peas, drained or 1 package | from cooking chicken |
| frozen, uncooked | 1  can carrots, drained |
| sugar to taste | |

Cook chicken, and cut into bite-size pieces. Spread over bottom of 13x9-inch pan that has been sprayed with Pam. Sprinkle peas and carrots over chicken. Mix the soups, broth, and sugar, and pour over chicken and vegetables.

**Topping:**

| | |
|---|---|
| 1  cup self-rising flour | 3/4  cup milk |
| 1  stick butter, melted | |

Combine ingredients, and pour over chicken and vegetable mixture. Bake, uncovered, for 45 minutes in a 400 degree oven.

*Jean Ann Bailey, Pearisburg, Virginia*

# Baked Peanut Butter Chicken

| | |
|---|---|
| 1  egg, beaten | 1/2  cup peanut butter |
| 1/2  cup mayonnaise | 1  Tablespoon milk |
| 1  teaspoon salt | 6  pieces chicken, skinned |
| wheat germ | |

Mix peanut butter, mayonnaise, milk, and salt with beaten egg. Dip chicken pieces into mixture; roll in wheat germ, and place in greased baking dish. Bake at 350 degrees for 1 hour.

# Chicken Cacciatore

| | |
|---|---|
| 2 pounds boneless chicken breasts | 2 small green peppers, chopped |
| 1 clove garlic, minced | salt and pepper |
| 2 Tablespoons pimento, chopped | 1 bay leaf |
| 1/4 teaspoon dried thyme | 6 sprigs parsley, chopped |
| 1 cup sliced mushrooms | 2 cups stewed tomatoes |

Combine all ingredients in sauce pan. Simmer 30 minutes. Uncover, and continue cooking until sauce is reduced to desired consistency. Serves 4.

*Mary S. Moss, Washington, North Carolina*

# Chicken Cashew

| | |
|---|---|
| 1/4 cup chopped onion | 1 cup chopped celery |
| 1 Tablespoon butter | 1 can mushroom soup, or less |
| 1/2 cup chicken broth | 1 Tablespoon soy sauce |
| 3 drops Tabasco | black pepper |
| 2 cups diced cooked chicken | 1 cup chow mein noodles |
| 1/2 cup cashew nuts | |

Sauté onion and celery in butter. Add mushroom soup, chicken broth, soy sauce, Tabasco, pepper, and cooked chicken. Simmer a few minutes. Pour into 1-quart casserole. Sprinkle top with chow mein noodles and cashew nuts. Bake in 350 degree oven for 20 minutes. Serves 4. Can be frozen without noodles and cashews. If frozen, add noodles and nuts after thawing and before baking.

*Mary S. Moss, Washington, North Carolina*

# Chicken Tetrazini

My children loved this dish. When Mother knew we were coming for a visit, she would prepare the tetrazini and freeze it in casseroles, in anticipation of our visit. This is a great way to use leftover turkey after a holiday. M.D.

| | |
|---|---|
| 2 boxes 1/4-inch noodles | 4 cans cream of mushroom soup |
| 4 cans cream of chicken soup | 1 1/2 pounds grated sharp cheese |
| 2 cups chicken broth | 1 clove garlic, or garlic salt |
| 1 medium onion, or onion salt | |
| 2 hens or 4 fryers, cooked | |

Cook noodles and drain. Sauté garlic and onions in a little butter. Add soups, broth, and 1/2 of cheese to onion and garlic. Stir, and heat until smooth. Add cut up chicken and noodles. Put in family-size casseroles for freezing. Top with other half of cheese. Bake in 350 degree oven until it bubbles (about 20 minutes).

*Mary S. Moss, Washington, North Carolina*

# Curried Chicken

| | |
|---|---|
| 1 large chicken | 2 Tablespoons butter |
| 1/2 cup chopped celery | 1 onion, sliced |
| 1 Tablespoon chopped parsley | 2 cups chicken stock |
| 2 teaspoons curry powder | 1 tomato, chopped |
| 1 tablespoon cornstarch | 1/2 cup cream |
| 2 cups cooked rice | salt to taste |
| small dish of chutney | 1 Tablespoon lemon juice |

Boil chicken until tender; cut into pieces. Brown onion in butter; add celery, parsley, salt, curry powder, stock, and tomato. Cook slowly for 30 minutes. Add cornstarch mixed with lemon juice. Add the cream and pieces of chicken. Reheat. Serve over rice, accompanied by dish of chutney.

# Seafood

# Baked Stuffed Shrimp

Great company dish! Can be prepared earlier in the day and refrigerated.
Large shrimp do just as well as the jumbo shrimp. M.D.

| | | | |
|---|---|---|---|
| 24 | raw jumbo shrimp, shelled and deveined | 2 | Tablespoons butter |
| 1/4 | cup minced celery | 1 | small onion, minced |
| 1 | Tablespoon chopped parsley | 1/2 | green pepper, minced |
| 1 | teaspoon salt | 1 | pound backfin crabmeat |
| 1/4 | teaspoon thyme | 1 | teaspoon Worcestershire |
| | dash Tabasco | | sauce |
| 1 | egg, beaten | 1/2 | cup seasoned bread crumbs |
| 1 | stick butter | 1 | cup light cream, or |
| | paprika | | milk |

Split shrimp lengthwise so they can be opened flat, but do not cut all the way
through. Spread flat in buttered shallow baking dish, and set aside. In the 2
tablespoons of butter, sauté onion, celery, and green pepper until onion is just
transparent. Remove from heat. Add parsley. Toss vegetable mixture with
crabmeat. Add seasonings, bread crumbs, egg, and cream. Toss gently.
Mound crab mixture on shrimp. Melt the stick of butter, and pour over the
shrimp. Sprinkle with paprika, and bake at 400 degrees for 15 minutes. This
can be prepared early in the day. If so, pour butter over shrimp just before
baking. Makes 6 servings.

# Seafood Casserole

| | |
|---|---|
| 1 pound lump crabmeat | 1 pound shrimp |
| 1 quart milk | 1/2 stick butter |
| 4 Tablespoons flour | 1/2 pound grated cheese |
| 1 Tablespoon Worcestershire sauce | salt and red pepper |

Cook, and peel shrimp. Cut into large pieces, and set aside. Make thick cream sauce from milk, butter, and flour. Add cheese, Worcestershire sauce, salt, and pepper to the hot cream sauce. Add crab and shrimp. Gently fold into sauce. Bake in casserole at 350 degrees for a short time. Top with grated cheese or cracker crumbs.

*Mary S. Moss, Washington, North Carolina*

# Shrimp Creole

| | |
|---|---|
| 1 pound fresh shrimp | 1 1/2 teaspoons salad oil, or butter |
| 1/2 cup chopped onions | |
| 1 clove garlic, chopped | 6 medium ripe tomatoes |
| 2 teaspoons salt | 1/8 teaspoon pepper |
| dash cayenne pepper | 2 bay leaves |
| 1/2 cup green pepper | |

Peel shrimp. Heat butter (or salad oil) in skillet. Add onions, garlic, and green pepper. Cook over slow heat, stirring occasionally. Peel tomatoes, and cut into quarters. Add to the above mixture; then add the salt, the 2 kinds of pepper, and the bay leaves. Cook over moderate heat for 10 minutes. Add shrimp, cover, and cook for 8 to 10 minutes. Remove bay leaves and serve over steamed rice.

*Mary S. Moss, Washington, North Carolina*

## Shrimp Scampi

24 large shrimp, shelled
and deveined
6 cloves garlic, crushed
1 teaspoon red pepper (optional)

1 cup lemon juice
1 cup olive oil
1 teaspoon chopped parsley

Wash shrimp in cold water. Dry, and arrange in pan. Mix the rest of the ingredients, and pour over shrimp. Let stand overnight in refrigerator. Next day, remove shrimp from marinade, place on broiler pan, and broil until brown. Heat 1/4 cup of the marinade to pour over shrimp when done.

## Crabmeat au Gratin

5 Tablespoons butter
1 cup milk
1 egg, well beaten
1 teaspoon salt
dash Tabasco
1 pound white lump crabmeat
1 cup Cheddar cheese, grated

3 Tablespoons flour
1 cup chicken boullion
2 Tablespoons sherry
1/4 teaspoon black pepper
1 Tablespoon Worcestershire
sauce

Make a white sauce of butter, flour, milk, boullion, and egg. Remove from heat; add wine, salt, pepper, Tabasco, and Worcestershire sauce. Add crab meat to white sauce, and put in 1 1/2 quart casserole . Sprinkle with cheese. Bake at 350 degrees for 20 minutes or until bubbly brown.

# Seafood Kebab

This is good served over rice or pasta with a salad and French bread or rolls. Jim enjoys preparing this for company and always gets compliments. The amount and variety of the seafood can be adjusted according to personal preference. M.D.

| | |
|---|---|
| butter or margarine | 3 medium shrimp per person |
| red wine vinegar dressing | 3 medium scallops per person |
| celery salt | 3 2-inch pieces of fish per |
| lemon pepper seasoning | person |
| lemon juice | 3 clams or oysters per person |
| green peppers | |
| onions (fresh or jar) | |
| tomatoes (cherry if available) | |
| mushrooms (optional) | |

Use a large, flat pan with deep sides. Line with heavy-duty aluminum foil. Butter the foil very thoroughly. Prepare the vegetables. If using fresh onions, peel and cut into quarters. If using processed onions, soak in vermouth until ready to use. Drain. Cut large tomatoes in half. Boil the fresh onions and peppers for 5 minutes. Peel the shrimp, and cut the fish into pieces. Arrange a single layer of seafood and vegetables in the pan. Sprinkle wine vinegar dressing, celery salt, lemon juice, and lemon pepper over the arrangement. Broil until seafood is cooked. If the oven is hot, it takes about 10 to 15 minutes. Don't overcook.

*Jim Darden, Virginia Beach, Virginia*

# Crab Soufflé

| | | | |
|---|---|---|---|
| 1 | pound crabmeat | 8 | slices white bread |
| | Miracle Whip | | celery |
| | salt | | red pepper |
| 4 | eggs | 2 | cups milk |
| 1 | can cream of mushroom soup | 1 | cup grated sharp Cheddar cheese |

Spread butter on 4 slices of bread. Trim crusts from bread, and cut into cubes. Grease bottom of 11x9-inch baking dish. Spread the bread cubes on bottom of dish. Make salad with crab, Miracle Whip, celery, salt, and red pepper. Butter, trim, and cube the other 4 slices of bread; spread on top of crab salad. Beat eggs with milk, and pour over entire casserole. Cover. Refrigerate 12 to 24 hours. Uncover. Bake in 350 degree oven for 15 minutes. Remove from oven, spread on mushroom soup, and sprinkle with grated cheese. Return to oven. Bake for 1 hour; cut into squares, and serve immediately. Makes 8 to 10 servings.

*Mary S. Moss, Washington, North Carolina*

# Crab and Shrimp Casserole

| | | | |
|---|---|---|---|
| 1 | clove garlic, chopped | 2 | Tablespoons butter |
| 2 | Tablespoons flour | 1 | cup milk |
| | salt and pepper to taste | 6 | dashes Tabasco |
| 2 | Tablespoons Worcestershire sauce | 1/2 | pound crabmeat |
| 1 | pound shrimp, peeled | 1/4 | pound sharp cheese, grated |

In a saucepan, sauté garlic in butter. Add all ingredients except cheese. Place in a 2-quart greased casserole, and sprinkle with grated cheese. Bake at 400 degrees for 20 minutes.

# Deviled Crab

Mother often served this in scallop shells. It also can be served in a casserole or ramekins. I have served it in a chafing dish with miniature pastry shells for a buffet. Regardless of how this crab dish is served, it is delicious and was one of Mother's favorites.   M.D.

| | | | |
|---|---|---|---|
| 2 | Tablespoons butter | 2 1/2 | Tablespoons flour |
| 1 | small can evaporated milk | | water |
| 2 | cups crabmeat | 1 | teaspoon salt |
| 1/4 | teaspoon paprika | | dash cayenne pepper |
| 2 | Tablespoons lemon juice | 1 | cup buttered bread crumbs |
| 1 | teaspoon Worcestershire sauce | 1 or 2 | hard boiled eggs |

Sprinkle the lemon juice, salt, paprika, and cayenne pepper on the crabmeat, and set aside. Make white sauce of flour, butter, and milk to which enough water has been added to make 1 1/2 cups liquid. Add Worcestershire sauce and chopped hard boiled eggs. Add crabmeat to sauce. Pour in buttered casserole, top with bread crumbs, and bake at 350 degrees for 15 to 18 minutes.

*Mary S. Moss, Washington, North Carolina*

# Crabmeat Casserole

| | | | |
|---|---|---|---|
| 1 1/4 | cups cooked crabmeat | 1 | can cream of celery soup |
| 1/4 | cup milk | 1/4 | cup salad dressing |
| 1 | cup cooked rice | | Cheddar cheese, shredded |

Heat (do not boil) soup, milk, and salad dressing. Add crabmeat and rice. Mix well. Pour into casserole dish; sprinkle cheese on top. Bake at 350 degrees until bubbly, approximately 20 minutes. Serves 6.

# Maryland Crabcakes

| | |
|---|---|
| 3 pounds crabmeat | 1 1/2 cups cracker crumbs |
| 6 Tablespoons mayonnaise | 3 Tablespoons prepared |
| 3 eggs, beaten | mustard |
| 3 Tablespoons parsley, chopped | 1 Tablespoon Worcestershire |
| butter | sauce |

Mix crabmeat with cracker crumbs. Mix mayonnaise, mustard, eggs, parsley, and Worcestershire sauce. Blend this carefully with crabmeat. Form into patties. Refrigerate. When ready to serve, pan fry in butter (or oil) until golden brown. Drain on paper towels. Serves 8. Can use 1 pound crabmeat and reduce other ingredients by one-third. Leftovers make good crabcake sandwiches the next day!

*Mary Stewart Darden, Virginia Beach, Virginia*

# Scalloped Oysters

| | |
|---|---|
| 1 pint shucked oysters | 2 cups cracker crumbs |
| 1/2 teaspoon salt | pepper to taste |
| 1/2 cup melted butter | dash Worcestershire sauce |
| 1 cup milk | |

Crumble enough saltine crackers to make 2 cups. Combine cracker crumbs, salt, pepper, and melted butter. Place a layer of this mixture in the bottom of a casserole. Cover with oysters. Repeat layers until all of the oysters are used. Add Worcestershire sauce to milk and pour over layered mixture. Bake at 350 degrees about 30 minutes.

# Oysters au Gratin

| | |
|---|---|
| 1 quart oysters, undrained | 1/4 cup butter |
| 1/4 cup flour | 1/2 teaspoon salt |
| 1/4 teaspoon pepper | 1/8 teaspoon nutmeg |
| 1/2 cup cream | serving shells, buttered |
| cracker crumbs | grated cheese |

Bring oysters to boiling point in own liquor, drain, save the liquid. Beat butter to a cream, add flour, salt, pepper, and nutmeg. Beat until smooth. Gradually dilute with one cup of warm oyster liquid. Return to saucepan, and as soon as the sauce boils, add cream. Return liquid to boil, and add oysters. Pour into shells, cover with buttered cracker crumbs, top with grated cheese, and bake at 375 degrees until crumbs are brown.

# Tuna Fish Noodles

| | |
|---|---|
| 1 small package noodles | 1 can mushroom soup |
| 3 hard boiled eggs, chopped | 1 can tuna fish |
| 1/2 cup milk | pimento or green pepper |
| bread crumbs | butter |

Heat soup and milk in saucepan. Add chopped eggs, cooked noodles, tuna fish, and a little pimento or green pepper. Mix gently. Pour in greased baking dish, dot with butter, and sprinkle with bread crumbs. Bake in 350 degree oven for 20 minutes.

 # Cooking Fish

To cook fish with less odor, squeeze lemon juice on the cleaned fish and chill in the refrigerator an hour before cooking.

# Baked Rock Fish

Wouldn't you think that having lived near the water most of my life, I would automatically be a lover of all kinds of seafood? Maybe, but with few exceptions, this has not proved to be true in my case. My grandfather owned oyster beds on the Elizabeth River when I was a child, but I can't remember having even tasted an oyster until well into my adult years. In fact, I don't remember wanting to taste shellfish of any kind until I became old enough to realize that I must be missing something. As for fish, I remember getting excited about eating fried spot but easily being able to pass up flounder. Today I still get excited about fried spot but, of course, shouldn't eat things fried. Unlike most folks, the fishier the taste of the fish, the better I like them. One real favorite of mine was, and is, baked rock fish, "the way Mother used to make it."   M.P.

|  | salt | 2 | Tablespoons flour |
|--|------|---|-------------------|
|  | pepper | 1 | medium onion, chopped |
| 4 to 5 | slices bacon | 1/2 | cup crackers, crumbled |
| 1 | teaspoon vinegar | 1 1/2 | cups water or more |
| 1 | 3- to 4-pound rock fish | | |

Clean fish; rub inside and out with salt, pepper, and flour. Place in large baking dish. Put half of chopped onion inside of fish and half on top. Mix vinegar with water, and pour into dish. (Water should be about 1/2 inch deep.) Cut bacon into small pieces, and fry. Pour drippings with fried bacon pieces over fish. Sprinkle crumbled crackers on top. Bake in 350 degree oven until fish is done. Baste often during baking.

*Alice Heath Taylor, Norfolk, Virginia*

# Baked Flounder

4 flounder fillets
4 strips bacon
   water

1 large onion, sliced
3 medium potatoes

Arrange fillets in bottom of buttered casserole. Place onion slices on fillets, and top each with a bacon strip. Add chunky potatoes which have been par-boiled. Add a little water. Cover with foil, and bake at 350 degrees for about 20 minutes.

*Mary S. Moss, Washington, North Carolina*

# Salmon Cakes

1 can salmon
1 teaspoon parsley flakes
2 Tablespoons cracker crumbs, crushed
2 Tablespoons vegetable oil

1 egg, slightly beaten
1 Tablespoon onion, minced
   salt and pepper to taste
   flour
   milk, if needed

Flake salmon. Blend in beaten egg, parsley flakes, onion, crushed crackers, salt, and pepper. If mixture is too dry, add a little milk. Form into patties, and coat with flour. Refrigerate if there is time (about 1 hour). Heat oil in frying pan, and cook until golden brown.

*Alice Heath Taylor, Norfolk, Virginia*

# For the Grill

## Beef Kebab

| | | | |
|---|---|---|---|
| 1 1/2 | pounds beef round, cubed | 2 | Tablespoons steak sauce |
| 1/2 | cup catsup | 2 | Tablespoons cider vinegar |
| 2 | Tablespoons Worcestershire sauce | 1/4 | cup water |
| | | 1 | teaspoon salt |
| 2 | Tablespoons oil | 2 | Tablespoons sugar |
| | tomato, green pepper, onions | | |

Place all ingredients except meat and vegetables in a sauce pan; heat to boiling. Pour over meat, and let stand several hours or overnight. String on skewers, alternating meat cubes with onion, green pepper pieces, and unskinned tomato wedges. Grill over a good bed of coals. Baste by brushing with reheated marinade. Use remaining liquid for sauce when serving. Makes 4 servings.

## Fish Supreme

| | | | |
|---|---|---|---|
| 1 | stick butter | 1 | cup barbecue sauce |
| | wine | | garlic salt |
| | fresh tuna fillets | | |

Combine butter, barbecue sauce, wine, and garlic salt in sauce pan, and heat until butter melts. Place fish on grill. Baste often with sauce. Cook 20 to 30 minutes or until fish is white throughout. Turn as often as needed.

*Jim Darden, Virginia Beach, Virginia*

# Bluefish

Our son Michael has been a real fisherman since he was about five years old. This bluefish recipe comes with a great (fish) story about two friends returning home from a fishing trip, an abandoned gill netter's truck, two 80-quart coolers filled with one to two-pound blues, and two tired but contented friends sleeping under the stars, lulled by the steady boom of waves on the moonlit sand of the Outer Banks. He likes to call it his "Taylor Blues" story. M.P.

| | | | |
|---|---|---|---|
| 1 | 1 to 2-pound fresh bluefish | 1 | large white onion, sliced |
| 1 | green pepper, sliced | 1 | hunk of butter |
| | salt and pepper | | beer |

Roll out a piece of aluminum foil twice as long as it is wide. Put the bluefish longways on the sheet, and fold it vertically all around him. Drop on the hunk of butter; shake on the salt and pepper. Top with onion and green pepper slices, and pour on the last sip of beer from the currently opened can. Fold down the foil, and for good measure, wrap him again so the beer doesn't leak out. Put him on a hot fire for about 10 minutes, flip him over, and by the time your newly opened beer is about half done, so is the fish. My affection for this meal is most likely tied to my memory of that adventurous night, but it is the kind of fish story that would make you want to go out and try it again.

*Michael Taylor Proffitt, Virginia Beach, Virginia*

**Helpful Tip**

To prevent sticking and for ease in cleaning, spray grill rack with non-stick vegetable spray before cooking.

# Shrimp on the Grill

| | |
|---|---|
| 1/3 cup lime juice | 1/4 teaspoon salt |
| 1/4 teaspoon pepper | 1/3 cup olive oil |
| 2 Tablespoons orange juice | 1 clove garlic, minced |
| 1 jalapeno pepper, optional | 2 Tablespoons cilantro, |
| 1 pound large shrimp, peeled | chopped |

Combine above ingredients except the shrimp into a sauce. Brush on shrimp as they cook on the grill.

# Barbecued Chicken

| | |
|---|---|
| 1/3 cup vinegar | 2/3 cup water |
| juice of 1/2 lemon | 1 Tablespoon brown sugar |
| dash Tabasco | 1/2 stick margarine |
| salt | pepper |
| 1 chicken, split | |

Make sauce on top of stove using above ingredients. Arrange chicken on grill. Baste and turn frequently until done.

# Baked Chicken for the Grill

| | |
|---|---|
| 1 chicken, whole | 2 Tablespoons honey |
| 1 Tablespoon Heinz 57 Sauce | |

Place chicken on rack in shallow baking pan. Cover with foil, and place on grill or use grill lid to cover chicken. Combine honey and Heinz 57; baste chicken during last 15 minutes of cooking.

*Don Proffitt, Virginia Beach, Virginia*

# Good Grilled Burgers

1 pound ground turkey
2 Tablespoons Worcestershire
   sauce
1 teaspoon prepared mustard
   pepper

1/4 cup onion, chopped
2 Tablespoons catsup
1 Tablespoon horseradish
   salt

Combine all ingredients. Mix well. Shape into 4 patties. Cook on grill over hot coals or medium heat. Cook until done but not dry.

# Barbecued Spare Ribs

1 onion, finely chopped
1/2 cup water
   salad oil
1/4 cup lemon juice
2 Tablespoons prepared
   mustard

2 Tablespoons Worcestershire
   sauce
1/4 cup brown sugar
1 8-ounce can tomato sauce
   salt and pepper
4 pounds spare ribs or
   back ribs

Cook ribs on grill rack over slow coals, turning often. In a saucepan, brown onions in oil until tender. Add remaining ingredients and simmer for 15 to 20 minutes. Baste ribs with sauce during the last 20 minutes of cooking time.

# Pickles, Relishes and Sauces

## Cottage at Emerald Isle

*I have always enjoyed the beach and have many fond memories of family vacations at Emerald Isle, N.C. The drawing of the cottage by my daughter reminds us of Emerald Isle. — M.D.*

# PICKLES, RELISHES, AND SAUCES
## Pickles

## Bread and Butter Cucumber Pickles

One of my early childhood memories is of spending summers in Charlotte at my grandfather's house. I remember the women in the kitchen making pickles with the cucumbers from the garden. I don't know how many people make pickles today, but I'm sure it must be easier in an air-conditioned kitchen! M.D.

| | | | |
|---|---|---|---|
| 1 | gallon cukes | 8 | small onions |
| 1/2 | cup salt | 5 | cups vinegar |
| 5 | cups sugar | 3 | Tablespoons white mustard |
| 1 | Tablespoon celery seed | | seed |
| 1/2 | teaspoon cloves | 1 1/2 | teaspoons tumeric |

Sprinkle salt over cukes and onions that have been cut into 1/2-inch slices. Soak in ice cubes for 3 hours. Drain, and dry thoroughly on towels. Combine remaining ingredients; bring to a boil. Add dried cukes and onions, and again bring to a boil. Immediately put into airtight jars, and seal.

*Mary S. Moss, Washington, North Carolina*

## Pickled Nasturtiums

Gather them young; lay them in salt and water one night. Drain; then cover with hot vinegar, boiled with a little black and Jamaica pepper. A couple of capsicums put into the jar will be a great improvement. (Comment: A capsicum is a kind of pepper.)

# Sweet Pickles

| | |
|---|---|
| 5 cups sugar | 4 1/2 teaspoons celery seed |
| 3 3/4 cups vinegar | 4 1/2 teaspoons tumeric |
| 3 Tablespoons salt | 1 teaspoon mustard seed |
| 15 cucumbers | |

Scrub cucumbers, and slice into 1/2-inch pieces. Place in a large container, and cover with boiling water. Leave overnight. Next morning, drain cucumbers, and put in jars. (15 cucumbers cut in 1/2-inch slices should fill 4 wide-mouth quart jars.) Combine remaining ingredients. Boil for 5 minutes. Pour over slices in jars, and seal. Place in a canner or large pot, and boil 5 minutes in a hot water bath. (Janie says her boys like these even better than Company Best pickles.)

*Janie Proffitt Flippo, Roanoke, Virginia*

# Sweet-Tart Pickles

| | |
|---|---|
| 1 large jar whole, dill pickles | white vinegar |
| sugar | |

Drain pickles, and rinse several times in cold water. Slice each pickle lengthwise into 8 pieces. Put pickles in jar; add sugar — about 1 1/2 cups for 1-quart jar. Put on lid, and shake. Fill jar 2/3 full with vinegar; put on lid and shake until sugar is dissolved. Sample liquid, and add more vinegar or sugar according to taste. Store in refrigerator for 3 days. Taste pickles. If pickles are not sweet enough, pour off some of the liquid, and add more sugar. Wait another 3 days, and taste again. Continue until pickles are crisp and sweet. If pickles are cut in slices lengthwise instead of in wedges, they fit nicely on sandwiches and taste wonderful. Juice from pickles may be used again, but a little more sugar and vinegar may need to be added.

*Jeanne Miller Proffitt, Pearisburg, Virginia*

# Universal Pickles

| | |
|---|---|
| 6 quarts vinegar | 1 pound salt, or less |
| 1 ounce cloves | 1 ounce allspice |
| 1 ounce ginger | 1 ounce black pepper |
| 1 Tablespoon cayenne pepper | 1 pound mustard |
| 1 ounce tumeric powder | vinegar |
| brown sugar | cucumbers |
| other vegetables | |

Combine vinegar, salt, cloves, allspice, ginger, black pepper, and cayenne pepper, and boil for 5 minutes. When cool, add the mustard and the tumeric, which has been dissolved in a little cold vinegar. Add brown sugar to taste. Add cucumbers and other tender vegetables. Use stone jar.

 ## Virginia Damson Pickles

To five pounds damsons allow five pounds of sugar and two and one-half pints vinegar. Take the vinegar and put to it two ounces mace, one ounce cinnamon and one ounce cloves. Let it come to a boil and pour over the fruit and sugar; cover close. Turn off and scald the syrup for six successive days; the seventh day let fruit, spices and all come to a boil. It will keep for years.

 ## Pickled Peppers

Cut out the stem of the peppers in a circle, and wash out in cold water; then fill each with a mixture of finely-chopped cabbage, horseradish, cucumbers and mustard seed; then replace the pieces cut from the top and sew around with coarse thread. Pack in stone jars and cover with cold vinegar.

## Watermelon Rind Pickles

| | |
|---|---|
| 7 pounds rind | 7 pounds sugar |
| 1 quart vinegar | 1 box ginger root |
| 1 box whole cloves | 1 box cinnamon bark |
| 1 box Lilly's lime | |

Cover rinds in lime water, and soak overnight. In the morning, rinse thoroughly, and cook until tender in clear water with ginger root that has been wrapped in a cloth. Rinds are tender when they can be pricked with a fork. Drain. Make a syrup of vinegar, sugar, and spices. The spices should be wrapped in cloth. Add 1 to 1 1/2 cups water to the vinegar mixture if it is too strong. Cook rind in syrup until syrup becomes as thick as you like it.

*Annie Harrell Stewart, Charlotte, North Carolina*

# Relishes

## Chow Chow (1939)

| | |
|---|---|
| 4 quarts cabbage | 2 quarts green tomatoes |
| 1 quart onions | 1 dozen green peppers |
| hot pepper to taste | 3 pints vinegar |
| 1 1/2 pounds white sugar | 1 cup flour |
| 1 Tablespoon tumeric | 2 Tablespoons dry mustard |
| 1 Tablespoon celery seeds | 3 Tablespoons salt |

Add sugar and celery seeds to 2 cups of the vinegar, and boil. Make a smooth paste of the flour, tumeric, mustard, and the last cup of vinegar. Mix into hot vinegar mixture, and cook a few minutes. Add vegetables, let boil 20 minutes, and can.

*Annie Harrell Stewart, Charlotte, North Carolina*

## Pepper Relish

| | |
|---|---|
| 1 dozen red peppers | 1 dozen green peppers |
| 1 dozen onions | hot peppers to taste |
| vinegar to cover | 1 cup brown sugar |
| 1 teaspoon salt | |

Bring to a boil.  Seal up.

*Annie Harrell Stewart, Charlotte, North Carolina*

 ## Salad Preparation

| | |
|---|---|
| 1 dozen green peppers | 4 dozen red peppers |
| 2 onions | 2 spoonfuls sugar |
| 1 cup vinegar | |

Boil 5 minutes, and can for use in winter for making salads.

*Annie Harrell Stewart, Charlotte, North Carolina*

 ## Picollilly

Four quarts each of cut cucumbers, beans and cabbage.  Two quarts each of cut peppers and onions and four quarts each of celery and nasturtiums.  Pour on boiling vinegar, flavored strongly with mustard, mustard seed and ground cloves.

# Sauces

## Chili Sauce

| | |
|---|---|
| 1 dozen ripe tomatoes | 1 dozen green tomatoes |
| 1/2 dozen onions | red pepper to taste |
| 1 Tablespoon allspice | 1 Tablespoon cloves |
| 1 Tablespoon nutmeg | 2 Tablespoons salt |
| 1 cup sugar | 1 quart vinegar |

Combine tomatoes, onions, and red pepper. Cook about 2 hours. Add allspice, cloves, nutmeg, salt, and sugar. Cook until very thick. Add vinegar, and remove from fire. Bottle when cool enough.

*Annie Harrell Stewart, Charlotte, North Carolina*

## Tomato Catsup

One-half bushel ripe tomatoes cut in halves; sprinkle with salt and leave them overnight. Drain off the juice, add one pint of water, and stew slowly in a large kettle till quite soft. Then put through a colander to free from skins. Return to the kettle and add one capful of salt, one-half ounce cayenne pepper, one ounce powdered cloves, one ounce each of nutmeg and mace. Simmer slowly for two or three hours, and add, when nearly cooked, one bottle of cooking wine. When quite cold, bottle and cork tight.

# Fondue Sauces

The following three recipes were given to me by a friend, Judy Ward, several years ago. My husband and I spent many wonderful, fun-filled evenings with Judy and Tom Ward. We would spend hours around the dinner table with a salad, a loaf of French bread, a plate of beef cubes, these delicious sauces, a fondue pot, and plenty of conversation. We still have the fondue pot and forks, and one of these days Jim and I hope to sit around the dinner table with the Wards and talk about old times while dipping into these sauces. M.D.

### Sweet and Sour

| | | | |
|---|---|---|---|
| 1 | cup sugar | 1/2 | cup white vinegar |
| 1/2 | cup water | 1/2 | teaspoon salt |
| 2 | teaspoons cornstarch | 1 | Tablespoon cold water |

Combine sugar, vinegar, water, and salt. Simmer 5 minutes. Add cornstarch that has been mixed in cold water. Cook and stir until mixture thickens.

### Garlic Butter

| | | | |
|---|---|---|---|
| 1 | stick butter | 1 | clove garlic |

Melt butter very slowly. Add finely chopped garlic, and simmer for about 5 minutes.

### Gaucho

| | | | |
|---|---|---|---|
| 1 | cup catsup | 1 | Tablespoon Worcestershire |
| 3 | dashes Tabasco | | sauce |
| 1/4 | cup vinegar | 1 | Tablespoon sugar |
| 1 | teaspoon salt | | |

Combine ingredients, and simmer for 30 minutes.

*Judy Ward, Tarboro, North Carolina*

# Barbecue

When anyone mentions REAL barbecue, I recall an occasion during a family visit to a friend's farm in Martin County, North Carolina. My father grew up in Martin County but moved to Norfolk in the 1920's. There was one special friend near Hassell whose family always welcomed us into their home.

On one extended weekend visit, my dad and his friend decided that some barbecue would taste mighty good, and in what seemed no time at all, a healthy size pig was selected for the feast. In good time, it was cleaned, skewered, and ready for roasting. Under a shelter near the barn, a pit was dug and the bottom was lined with hot coals. The cooking began during the chilly, dark hours of night, but the heat from the pit kept the men warm. By the time we children were up and stirring, the meat was browning to perfection. The aroma was hard-to-wait tempting, but we knew that REAL barbecue couldn't be hurried. Finally, after just the right number of hours, the confection was sizzling juicily to let the cooks know that it was done through and through.

The now succulent pig was moved to a large table that had been scrubbed shining clean. There, the carving, chopping, and final seasoning took place. It was hard work, but soon there was such an inviting scent in the air that we on-lookers were not above snitching a taste or two to voice our expert opinions. And, by the way, let me tell you that not even for a split second was a tomato-type barbecue sauce considered for seasoning on this pig. Not in this part of North Carolina!

After the last of the coals had died out and the taste-testers had declared the barbecue to be *perfect,* the delectable treasure was divided among those who had helped in any way with its preparation. There was plenty for all.

This event is one of my favorite things to recall from those days of long ago. The memory of it has always served well to let me know when I'm eating REAL NORTH CAROLINA BARBECUE! M.P.

# Barbecue Sauce No. 1

Our friends in North Carolina no longer keep hogs on their farm, so their barbecuing is done on a much smaller scale.  M.P.

| | |
|---|---|
| 1  fresh pork shoulder or ham | hot pepper vinegar |
| black  pepper | cayenne pepper |
| salt | |

To make hot pepper vinegar, finely chop hot peppers, and let soak in vinegar for about 2 weeks.  (Peppers may be included in the sauce or may be removed from the vinegar before mixing with the cooked pork.)  Bake the fresh pork ham or shoulder.  Remove meat from the bone; chop, and season with sauce made from pepper vinegar, black pepper, cayenne pepper, and salt.

*Selma Jean Everett, Hassell, North Carolina*

# Barbecue Sauce No. 2

| | |
|---|---|
| 1/3  cup vinegar | 2/3  cup water |
| juice of 1/2 lemon | 1  Tablespoon brown sugar |
| 1/2  stick margarine | Tabasco |
| salt | pepper |

Combine ingredients, and simmer until flavors meld.

# Barbecue Sauce No. 3

| | |
|---|---|
| 1  pint apple cider vinegar | 1  Tablespoon salt |
| 1  teaspoon pepper | 1  teaspoon cayenne  pepper |
| 1  Tablespoon prepared mustard | 2  Tablespoons catsup |
| 1  teaspoon paprika | 1  Tablespoon fresh lemon juice |

Mix all ingredients, and bring to a boil over low heat.  Stir constantly.  Remove from heat and strain.  Cool.

# Shrimp Sauce

Every summer from the late 1960's until the late 1970's, we would have a small family reunion at Atlantic Beach or Emerald Isle. My parents and Mother's sister would rent a house for a week at the beach. My uncle and aunt would have a house close by. All of us have wonderful memories of those summers. Everyone always looked forward to Uncle Robert's sauce and the North Carolina shrimp. If the shrimp ran out, we would put the sauce on crackers. M.D.

| | |
|---|---|
| 1 pint Miracle Whip | 1/2 bottle catsup |
| 1 bottle chili sauce | 2 teaspoons prepared |
| 1 bottle cream style horseradish | mustard |
| relish (India or other sweet) | Worcestershire sauce |
| salt | black pepper |
| Texas Pete, if desired | 1 medium onion |

Grate the onion, and combine with other ingredients.

*Robert Stewart, Shallotte, North Carolina*

 # Pear Honey

| | |
|---|---|
| 7 pounds pears | 5 pounds sugar |
| 1 No. 2 can crushed pineapple | juice of 1 lemon |

Cook pears until tender, and add pineapple. Cook until thick. Maraschino cherries may be added with pineapple if desired. Makes 7 or 8 pints.

# Salads

## The Porch in Summer

*Porches offered a relief from the heat of the summer and
provided a gathering place for family and friends —
a tradition of Southern hospitality. — M.D.*

# SALADS

## Grapefruit Salad

Refreshing and light! I often use individual molds or prepare the salad in a flat
Pyrex dish and cut into squares to serve. M.D.

| | |
|---|---|
| 5 large grapefruit | 4 packages lemon jello |
| 8 cups chopped grapefruit sections and juice | 1 can crushed pineapple, if desired |
| pinch of salt | 4 cups boiling water |

Cut grapefruit in halves, cut out sections, and discard bitter pulp. Dissolve
jello in 4 cups boiling water. Add grapefruit sections with juice, pineapple with
juice, and salt. Fill halves, and let congeal. When ready to serve, cut into
quarters and pour the special dressing over it. Recipe can be reduced.

**Dressing**:

| | |
|---|---|
| 3 egg yolks | 1/3 cup sugar |
| pinch salt | 3 Tablespoons flour |
| 3 Tablespoons lemon juice | 1 cup pineapple juice |
| 12 marshmallows | 1 pint whipped cream |
| 1 cup almonds, blanched and chopped | |

Combine egg yolks, sugar, salt, flour, lemon juice, and pineapple juice and
cook in a double boiler until thick. While hot, add marshmallows. Heat again;
then cool. Add whipped cream and almonds. Dressing may be prepared the
day before except for adding the cream and almonds. Makes 20 servings.

*Mary S. Moss, Washington, North Carolina*

# Grapefruit Date Salad

My grandmother had 1929 written on this recipe!  M.D.

| | |
|---|---|
| sliced dates | grapefruit sections |
| 1/2  cup oil | 1  teaspoon salt |
| 1/4  cup grapefruit juice | 1/4  teaspoon paprika |

Place a mound of sliced dates on a leaf of lettuce.  Surround with grapefruit sections.  Place the oil, grapefruit juice, salt, and paprika in a covered container.  Shake until well blended.  Pour this dressing over the salad.  Serves 6.

*Annie Harrell Stewart, Charlotte, North Carolina*

# Bridge Salad

| | |
|---|---|
| juice of 2 oranges | juice of 1 lemon |
| 3  egg yolks, slightly beaten | 2  teaspoons corn starch |
| 1  Tablespoon butter | 4  Tablespoons sugar |
| 1  envelope unflavored gelatin | 1/2  pint whipped cream |
| 1  cup pineapple pieces | 4  ounces chopped pecans |
| 1/2  apple, grated | 1/2  cup maraschino cherries, |
| water | chopped |

Combine orange and lemon juices, egg yolks, cornstarch, butter, and sugar.  Cook in double boiler until thick..  Dissolve gelatin in 1/2 cup cold water.  Add to juice mixture.  Let cool.  When cooled and the mixture begins to thicken, add whipped cream, pineapple, nuts, apple, and cherries.  Pour into large ring mold or any serving container suitable for a gelatin salad.

# Autumn Apple Salad

Most of the recipes in this book are from Virginia or North Carolina, but I couldn't pass up the opportunity to include one given to me by my good golfing buddy and close friend Sharon. She brought it to me when she returned from a family reunion in Nebraska in 1995. It sounds scrumptious, and I am happy that we can now claim it as a local recipe. M.P.

| | | | |
|---|---|---|---|
| 1 | 20-ounce can crushed pineapple, undrained | 2/3 | cup sugar, or 8 packets artificial sweetener |
| 1 | 3-ounce package lemon jello | 1 | 8-ounce package cream cheese |
| 1 | cup celery, chopped | | |
| 1 or 2 | cups diced apples unpeeled | 1/2 to 1 | cup nuts, chopped |
| | | 1 | cup whipped topping |

In saucepan, combine undrained pineapple and sugar. Bring to a boil, and continue to boil for 3 minutes. Add jello (do not add water). Stir until dissolved. Add softened cream cheese, and blend thoroughly into mixture. Cool. Fold in apples, nuts, celery, and topping. Pour into 9-inch square pan or large bowl. Chill until firm. "Lite" cream cheese and "lite" whipped topping may be substituted for heavier type ingredients. Enjoy!

*Sharon Haring, Virginia Beach, Virginia*

# Cherry Salad

| | | | |
|---|---|---|---|
| 1 | No. 2 can red sour cherries | 1 | package cherry jello |
| 1 | small can crushed pineapple | 1 | cup nuts, chopped |
| 1/3 | cup sugar | | |

Put can of cherries (juice and all) in pan. Add 1/3 cup sugar, let come to a boil. Remove from stove, and sprinkle cherry jello over this mixture. Do not use any water with the jello. Let cool slightly. Add nuts and pineapple (juice and all).

*Genevieve Proffitt, Salisbury, Maryland*

# Bing Cherry Salad

Once when Mother served this salad, a spoonful fell on the kitchen floor. Our dachshund, Cricket, quickly rushed over to eat the salad. My sister and I took great delight in teasing Mother, telling her that the dog was feeling the effects of the wine salad. Mother was not amused, but Cricket was delighted with all the attention. M.D.

| | |
|---|---|
| 1 can cherries, pitted | 1 package dark cherry jello |
| 1 cup nuts, or less | 1 cup port wine |
| lemon juice | |

Drain juice from cherries, and add enough water to make 1 cup. Heat this to boiling, and pour over jello. Dissolve jello thoroughly. Add port wine, nuts, and a spoonful or two of lemon juice. This makes about 6 individual molds.

*Mary S. Moss, Washington, North Carolina*

# Christmas Salad

| | |
|---|---|
| 2 packages strawberry jello | 2 cups boiling water |
| 2 10-ounce packages frozen strawberries | 1 1/2 cups crushed pineapple, drained |
| 2 ripe bananas | 1 cup sour cream |

Dissolve jello in boiling water. Add frozen berries, and stir slowly until thawed. Add pineapple and bananas to mixture. Pour half the mixture into serving dish. Chill until firm. Spread sour cream evenly over chilled jello mixture. Add remaining gelatin mixture, and chill until firm..

# Spiced Peach Salad

1 teaspoon cloves
1 large jar pickled peaches
1 teaspoon plain gelatin
1 package lemon jello
dash lemon juice

1/4 cup water
2 cups liquid
1 Tablespoon cold water
pinch salt

Boil cloves in 1/4 cup water for 5 minutes. Strain into measuring cup. Cut up peaches; reserve juice. Soak gelatin in tablespoon of cold water. Set aside. Combine peach juice, spice liquid, and enough water to make 2 cups. Bring to boil; add gelatin and jello. Stir until dissolved. Return cut up peaches to liquid; add a pinch of salt and dash of lemon juice. Pour into molds that have been rinsed with cold water. May be made several days ahead.

*Mary S. Moss, Washington, North Carolina*

# Pineapple Marshmallow Salad

3 eggs
1 cup sugar
1 large bag miniature
marshmallows

1/2 cup vinegar
1 can pineapple chunks
1/2 cup nuts
1/2 pint whipping cream

Beat eggs well; add sugar. Cook in a double boiler adding vinegar a little at a time. Stir well while cooking. When thick enough to peak, let cool. Pour over pineapple, nuts, and marshmallows. Mix well. Whip the cream, and fold in. Chill in refrigerator. Can be served on lettuce as salad, or without lettuce as dessert.

*Mary S. Moss, Washington, North Carolina*

# Frozen Fruit Salad

When I made this salad to take to a Darden Christmas dinner several years ago, it was so popular my mother-in-law asked me to make the salad every Christmas after that. She suggested doubling the amount of whipping cream and omitting the mayonnaise. It is delicious that way too! When I make a large quantity of this salad, I use 9x13-inch pans. This makes it easier to cut into squares and serve. M.D.

| | | | | |
|---|---|---|---|---|
| 1 | pint cream | 6 | bananas, sliced |
| 1 | pint mayonnaise | 1/2 | pound Wisconsin cheese, grated |
| 1 | lemon | | |
| 1 | cup nuts, chopped | 2 | small packages cream cheese |
| 1 | pound sugar | 1 | can pears, large |
| 1 | small bottle cherries | 1 | can crushed pineapple, large |
| 2 | large cans fruit salad | | |

Put pineapple and juice over sugar, and let stand. Drain all other fruit. Mix mayonnaise and grated cheese. Add softened cream cheese. Sprinkle lemon juice on bananas. Combine all fruit and nuts with mayonnaise mixture. Whip cream, and fold into mixture. Freeze in ice trays or oyster cartons. Will keep a couple of months. Serves 25.

*Mary S. Moss, Washington, North Carolina*

# Apricot Salad

| | | | | |
|---|---|---|---|---|
| 1 | large package apricot gelatin | 1 | medium can crushed pineapple |
| 1 1/2 | cups cheddar cheese, shredded | 1 | large container Cool Whip |

Mix 2 cups boiling water with jello. Add 6 or 7 ice cubes, stir until dissolved. Beat with mixer. Blend in pineapple and cheese. Beat with mixer. Fold in whipped topping. Chill until set.

# Delicious Summer Fruit Salad

Ah! Summer in Virginia Beach where golf outings, art shows, beach parties, and picnics are regular forms of entertainment. Almost any excuse works for getting folks together, and this is a truly refreshing summer taste treat for any occasion. M.P.

| | | | |
|---|---|---|---|
| 1 | cantaloupe | 1 | honeydew melon |
| 1 | pint watermelon | 4 | fresh peaches |
| 1 | pint strawberries | 4 | large bananas |
| 5 | Tablespoons Fruit Fresh | 2/3 | cup sugar |

Sprinkle Fruit Fresh on fruit that has been cut into cubes or made into melon balls. Gently mix in sugar. Fold the dressing into the fruit just before serving.

**Dressing:**
Make dressing the day before serving.

| | | | |
|---|---|---|---|
| 3/4 | cup apple juice | 3/4 | cup orange juice |
| 1 | cup sugar | 4 | Tablespoons cornstarch |
| 1 | Tablespoon poppy seeds | | |

Mix sugar and cornstarch with enough apple and orange juice to dissolve. Add rest of juice, and heat until thickened. Add poppy seeds. Let dressing cool, and store in refrigerator overnight.

# Angel Salad

| | | | |
|---|---|---|---|
| 1/4 | pound small marshmallows | 1 | small package cream cheese |
| 1 | small can crushed pineapple | 1/2 | pint whipped topping |
| 1/2 | cup nuts | 1 | small package lime jello |

Dissolve jello, marshmallows, and cream cheese in boiling water according to jello directions. Chill until almost firm; add pineapple, whipped topping, and nuts. Mix well and chill until firm.

# Heavenly Hash

Many years ago, soon after Don and I were married, I was introduced to the family tradition of spending a week in a rented cabin at Douthat State Park near Clifton Forge, Virginia, Don's home town. His folks had gone there each summer for years. In fact, a couple of brothers had helped build the place. Our own family became regulars too, as we took our sons there several summers running during the 60's. They still talk about Cabin 17 or Cabin 12 or any of their other "favorite cabins." We were last there in 1992, when we had a huge family reunion at the Guest Lodge. My sweet sister-in-law "Sis" introduced me to Heavenly Hash during our very first trip to Douthat. That was a long time ago, and both the recipe and the sister-in-law have remained as sweet ever since. M.P.

| | | | |
|---|---|---|---|
| 2 | cans mandarin oranges | 2 | cans pineapple chunks |
| 1 | can shredded coconut | 1 | small bag miniature |
| 1 | carton sour cream | | marshmallows |

Drain juice off fruits. Mix fruit pieces, coconut, and sour cream together. Chill.

*"Sis" Waid Proffitt, Salisbury, Maryland*

# Pineapple Nut Salad

| | | | |
|---|---|---|---|
| 1 | small package lime jello | 1 | cup boiling water |
| 1 | can (No.2) crushed pineapple | 1/2 | cup nuts |
| 1 | cup cottage cheese | | sour cream |
| | nutmeg | | |

Mix jello in boiling water. Stir until dissolved. Mix in pineapple, nuts, and cottage cheese. Chill until firm. Top with sour cream mixed with a little nutmeg.

# Blueberry Salad

1   6-ounce box cherry gelatin
1   cup cold water
1   small can crushed pineapple, drained
1/2   cup chopped nuts

2   cups boiling water
1   can blueberry pie filling
1   3 1/2-ounce package cream cheese
1   4-ounce Cool Whip

Mix boiling water with gelatin, and stir until dissolved.  Add cold water, pineapple, nuts, and pie filling.  Chill until firm.  Beat Cool Whip and cream cheese together, and spread over top of firm gelatin salad.

# Watergate Salad

This is a well-known recipe, but I include it because it came to me from a fellow librarian with whom I worked many years ago at Independence Junior High School.  I particularly recall eating this always delicious treat during a spectacular snow storm in Virginia Beach during the 70's.  Several couples from Independence had planned to get together for dinner at Donald and Loretta Bishop's home in the Seagate Condominium, and, by golly, no mere 2 or 3 feet of snow were going to stop us.  Each of us brought something to make the pot lucky, and I'm sure this dish was present.  Whenever I prepare it, I think of the good times shared by that wonderful group of friends.  M. P.

1   20-ounce can crushed pineapple
1   3-ounce box pistachio pudding mix

1   container whipped topping

Mix dry pudding mix and crushed pineapple (do not drain).  Add whipped topping, and fold in well.  Chill.  (Can also add small marshmallows.)

*"Pete" Hughey, Virginia Beach, Virginia*

# Asparagus Salad

| | | | |
|---|---|---|---|
| 2 | envelopes gelatin | 1/2 | cup cold water |
| 3/4 | cup sugar, or less | | salt |
| 1/2 | cup white vinegar | 1 | cup water |
| 1/4 | cup asparagus juice | 1 | cup celery, chopped |
| 1/2 | cup pecans, chopped | 1 | can green asparagus |
| 1 | small can sliced pimentos | | juice of 1/2 lemon |
| 1 | Tablespoon onion, grated | | |

Dissolve gelatin in cold water. Combine sugar, vinegar, water, and salt, and bring to a boil. Continue boiling for 5 minutes. Remove from heat; add gelatin mixture; stir, and let cool. Combine remaining ingredients, and add to cooled liquid mixture. Chill until firm. Serves 6 to 8.

# Beet Salad

| | | | |
|---|---|---|---|
| 1 | 1-pound can shoestring beets | 1/2 | cup celery, chopped |
| 1 | 3-ounce package lemon jello | 1/4 | cup sugar |
| 1/4 | cup apple cider vinegar | 1/2 | teaspoon salt |
| 2 | teaspoons onion, grated | 1 | heaping Tablespoon horseradish or to taste |

Drain beets. Add water to make 1 1/2 cups liquid. Bring to a boil. Remove from heat, and add jello, sugar, vinegar, celery, onion, salt, beets, and horseradish. Let congeal.

*Dot Denton, Virginia Beach, Virginia*

# Broccoli Salad No. 1

| | |
|---|---|
| 2 heads broccoli, chopped | 1/2 cup raisins |
| 1/2 cup onions, chopped | 1 cup mayonnaise |
| 2 to 3 Tablespoons vinegar | 8 slices bacon, crumbled |

Combine all ingredients except bacon the night before serving. Fry, and crumble bacon. Add to other ingredients 10 to 15 minutes before serving.

*Debby Gooch, Virginia Beach, Virginia*

# Carolina Cole Slaw

| | |
|---|---|
| 1 large cabbage, grated or chopped | 1 green pepper, finely |
| 1 onion, finely chopped | chopped |

Combine cabbage, green pepper, and onion. Set aside.

**Dressing:**

| | |
|---|---|
| 1 cup sugar | 1 teaspoon salt |
| 1 teaspoon dry mustard | 1 teaspoon celery seed |
| 1 cup cider vinegar | 2/3 cup oil |

Mix sugar, salt, mustard, and celery seed in a saucepan. Add vinegar and oil; let come to a boil over moderate heat, stirring until sugar dissolves. Pour over cabbage mixture. Toss well to mix. Cover, and refrigerate. Will keep a week.

*Mary S. Moss, Washington, North Carolina*

# Broccoli Salad No. 2

| | |
|---|---|
| 4 cups broccoli flowerets | 1/2 cup carrots |
| 1/3 cup red onion | 1 Tablespoon Hormel Bacon |
| 1/2 cup dressing (Marie's Tangy | Bits |
| French or Kraft Catalina with | 1/4 cup raisins |
| Honey) | 3/4 cup cashews |

Cut broccoli, carrots, and onion into bite size pieces. Combine all ingredients except raisins and cashews. They should be mixed in just before serving. (If using Marie's Dressing, 1 tablespoon of sugar should be added.)

*"Corky" Proffitt Bailey, Pearisburg, Virginia*

# Old-Fashioned Cucumbers

| | |
|---|---|
| 1 medium cucumber | 2 small green peppers |
| 2 Tablespoons distilled | 1 Tablespoon sugar |
| white vinegar | 1 teaspoon salt |

Pare cucumber, and slice thin. Cut green peppers into thin strips. Stir together vinegar, sugar, and salt. Add cucumber and green pepper. Mix. Cover, and chill, stirring occasionally before serving. Makes 4 servings.

# Colorful Cole Slaw

| | |
|---|---|
| 1 head red cabbage, shredded | 1 head green cabbage, shredded |
| 1/2 dozen radishes, finely chopped | 1 carrot, shredded |
| 1/2 cup mayonnaise, or more | 1/4 cup sugar |
| 1/4 cup crushed pineapple, drained | 1 Tablespoon pineapple juice |

Set aside a small portion of radishes and carrots. Mix all other ingredients. Spoon into serving bowl, and garnish with rest of radishes and carrots. Refrigerate until well chilled. Serves 8 to 10.

# Harvey House Slaw

Talk about a cook!  My sister-in-law Janie can cook as well as her mother
Mae, who was the best cook ever.  I can't tell you how many times I have
overdosed on Janie's Lemon Pound Cake.  She is a real sweetheart who takes
special joy in cooking all day long and then takes more special joy in loading
everything she has cooked into her car and delivering it to friends and relatives.
We will always remember our family reunions for the wonderful rolls, turkeys,
pies, pole beans, etc., etc., etc. contributed by Janie.  Once when we were on
our way to a family get-together, we passed her stopped car on the highway.
She had the lid of her trunk open and was bending over a pan, punching down
the bread dough so it would be ready for making rolls when she arrived.  We
still get a laugh when we recall that episode.  This Harvey House slaw, however, is no laughing matter.  It's more of a swooning matter.  Sooooo good!
M.P.

| | |
|---|---|
| 1  large or 2 small heads green cabbage | 2  Bermuda onions |
| | 2  cups sugar |

Shred cabbage finely, as on a kraut cutter.  Put layer of cabbage in large bowl.
Top with a layer of onions; then green pepper if desired.  Alternate layers until
all vegetables are used.  Sprinkle sugar over top.  Do not stir.

**Dressing:**

| | |
|---|---|
| 4  teaspoons sugar | 1  teaspoon dry mustard |
| 1  cup vinegar | 1  teaspoon celery seed |
| 3/4  cup vegetable oil | 1  teaspoon salt |

Mix the dressing ingredients.  Bring to a boil.  Pour immediately over the
cabbage, and cover container tightly to hold steam.  Again, do not stir.  Refrigerate, and let stand at least 4 hours or longer.  Stir well, and serve.  Keeps as
long as it lasts.

*Janie Proffitt Flippo, Roanoke, Virginia*

# Sauerkraut Salad

| | | |
|---|---|---|
| 1 | large jar sauerkraut | 3/4 cup sugar |
| 1/2 | cup apple cider vinegar | 1 cup celery, chopped |
| 1 | cup green pepper, chopped | 1/4 cup onion, chopped |
| 1 | teaspoon celery seed | 1/4 teaspoon pepper |

Rinse sauerkraut and let drain.  Mix other ingredients with drained sauerkraut.

*Dot Denton, Virginia Beach, Virginia*

# Corn Salad

| | | |
|---|---|---|
| 2 | cups sweet corn, cooked | 3/4 cup fresh tomatoes, chopped |
| 1/2 | cup green pepper, chopped | 1/2 cup celery, chopped |
| 1/4 | cup green onion, chopped | 1/4 cup prepared ranch salad dressing |

In large salad bowl, combine vegetables.  Stir in dressing.  Cover, and refrigerate until serving.

*Dot Denton, Virginia Beach, Virginia*

# Congealed Cucumber Salad

| | | |
|---|---|---|
| 1 | package lime jello | 1 cup hot water |
| 2 | Tablespoons vinegar | 1 Tablespoon onion, minced |
| 1 1/2 | cups minced cucumber | 1/4 teaspoon salt. |
| 1/2 | cup mayonnaise | |

Dissolve jello in hot water.  Add vinegar and minced onion.  Chill until partially
thickened.  Mix minced cucumber with salt.  Drain well.  Whip gelatin until
fluffy.  Fold in mayonnaise and cucumber mixture.  Chill until firm.  (Finely
chopped celery may be added if desired.)

*Mary S. Moss, Washington, North Carolina*

# Beet Cucumber Salad Ring

| | | | |
|---|---|---|---|
| 1 | 16-ounce can shoestring beets | 1 | envelope unflavored gelatin |
| 1/4 | cup sugar | | dash salt |
| 3 | Tablespoons lemon juice | 1/2 | small cucumber, thinly sliced |
| | lettuce | | |

Drain beets, reserving liquid. Set aside. In small saucepan, combine gelatin, sugar, and salt. Add enough water to beet liquid to make 1 3/4 cups liquid. Add to gelatin mixture. Cook, and stir over low heat until gelatin dissolves. Stir in lemon juice. Pour about 3/4 cup of the gelatin mixture into a 3 1/2- or 4- cup ring mold. Arrange cucumber slices in bottom of mold. Chill both gelatin mixtures until larger amount is partially set. Stir drained beets into larger amount of gelatin. Spoon over cucumbers in mold. Chill until firm. Unmold onto lettuce-lined serving plate. Makes 6 servings.

# Mother's Potato Salad

Cook potatoes in skins. Peel, and cut up while warm. Add salt and a little grated onion (pepper, if desired). Add real mayonnaise and Durkee dressing while potatoes are warm. Refrigerate for several hours — or overnight. Add celery and green pepper (celery seed, if desired). Refrigerate again for several hours or overnight.

*Mary S. Moss, Washington, North Carolina*

 # Sweet Pickle Juice

When the sweet pickle jar is empty, save the juice and use it instead of vinegar when preparing salads.

# Day-Before Salad

This recipe is not original with my husband Don, but he prepares it beautifully. Often it is a specially requested menu item when we get together for a cook-out with friends.  M.P.

| | |
|---|---|
| 1   10-ounce package peas, frozen | 1   jar red wine and vinegar |
| 1   large head lettuce |      salad dressing |
| 1   green pepper, chopped | 1   cup onion, chopped |
| 3   stalks celery, thinly sliced | 1/2  pound bacon |
| 1   small jar black olives, sliced | 1/2  cup Cheddar cheese, |
| 3   large tomatoes, diced |      shredded |
|     mayonnaise | |

Combine peas, lettuce, pepper, onion, and celery.  Place in 13x9x2-inch glass dish.  Spread a little or lots of mayonnaise on top, however you choose. Sprinkle cheese over top.  Cover, and refrigerate overnight.  In separate container, combine tomatoes with 1/2 bottle of wine and vinegar salad dressing. Refrigerate overnight.  Stir occasionally.  Fry bacon, and crumble.  Before serving, spoon tomatoes and dressing mixture over salad.  Top with crumbled bacon and black olives.  No other dressing is needed.  (Any kind of cheese may be used; we usually use Cheddar.)

# Summer Salad

| | |
|---|---|
| 2   cups cooked macaroni | 2   cups diced tomatoes |
| 1   cup mayonnaise | 1   cup cheese |

Combine all ingredients.  Chill.  Add any other things preferred, shredded cabbage, etc.

*Annie Harrell Stewart, Charlotte, North Carolina*

# Carolina Tangy Vegetable Salad

| | |
|---|---|
| 3/4 cup vinegar | 3/4 cup sugar |
| 1 teaspoon salt | 1/2 teaspoon pepper |
| 1 Tablespoon water | 1 17-ounce can sweet peas, drained |
| 1 12-ounce can shoe peg corn, drained | 1 cup onion, chopped |
| 1 cup celery, chopped | 1 2-ounce jar pimentos |

Combine vinegar, sugar, salt, pepper, and water. Boil 1 minute; then cool.
Add peas, corn, celery, onion, and pimentos. Stir. Place in covered container,
and cool overnight. Serve chilled. Serves 8.

*June Hand-Decker, Virginia Beach, Virginia*

# Molded Vegetable Salad

| | |
|---|---|
| 2 packages lemon jello | 2 Tablespoons chili sauce |
| 1/4 cup green pepper, chopped | 1/4 cup olives, chopped |
| pimento, chopped | 1 cup nuts or less, chopped |
| 1 cup celery, chopped | 3 Tablespoons India relish |
| dash red pepper | dash salt |
| 1 1/2 cups boiling water | |

Add boiling water to jello, and set aside. Add all ingredients to jello when it
has cooled. Place in serving container. Serves 8. Is colorful, sweet, and tart.

*Mary S. Moss, Washington, North Carolina*

# Exotic Chicken Salad

| | |
|---|---|
| 1 quart chicken, cooked | 1 can water chestnuts |
| 1 pound seedless red or green grapes | 1 cup celery, sliced |
| 1 1/2 cups mayonnaise | 1 cup slivered almonds, toasted |
| 1 1/2 teaspoon curry powder | 1 Tablespoon soy sauce |
| Tablespoon lemon juice | 1 can pineapple chunks |
| Boston or bibb lettuce | |

Cook chicken, and cut into bite-sized pieces. Drain and slice water chestnuts. Combine with chicken, grapes, celery, and 1/2 cup of the almonds. Mix mayonnaise, curry powder, soy sauce, and lemon juice. Combine with chicken, and chill. Spoon onto a bed of lettuce leaves. Sprinkle with the rest of the almonds, and garnish with pineapple chunks.

# Oriental Chicken Salad

| | |
|---|---|
| 2 cups chicken | 1 can fancy mixed Chinese vegetables |
| 2 Tablespoons onion, chopped | |
| 1 cup celery, thinly sliced | 1/2 cup green pepper, chopped |
| 1 teaspoon salt | |
| 2 teaspoons soy sauce | 3/4 cup mayonnaise |

Cook and dice chicken. Drain and rinse Chinese vegetables. Combine ingredients. Toss, and chill. Water chestnuts may be added if desired.

*Sara Moss McCowen, Richmond, Virginia*

# Hawaiian Mayonnaise

Combine 2/3 cups mayonnaise and 3 tablespoons pineapple juice. Serve on fruit salads.

# Chunky Chicken

| | | | |
|---|---|---|---|
| 10 | chicken thighs | 2 | Tablespoons chicken broth |
| 1 | cup celery, chopped | 1/2 | cup sweet salad cubed |
| 2 | Tablespoons lemon juice | | pickles |
| 1 | small onion, grated | 1 | 8-ounce can water |
| 2 | teaspoons spicy brown | | chestnuts, thinly sliced |
| | mustard | 1/2 | cup mayonnaise |

Cut cooked, boned chicken thighs into 1/2-inch chunks. Mix chicken broth, celery, pickle, lemon juice, onion, water chestnuts, mustard, and mayonnaise. Add to chicken chunks. Chill for at least one hour. Serves 6

# Crab Salad

| | | | |
|---|---|---|---|
| 1 | pound crab meat | 2 | boiled eggs, chopped |
| 1 | stalk celery, chopped | 1 | medium onion, chopped |
| 1/2 | cup mayonnaise | 1 | teaspoon salt |
| 1/2 | teaspoon black pepper | | lettuce |

Combine all ingredients, and serve on bed of lettuce.

# Fresh Shrimp Salad

| | | | |
|---|---|---|---|
| 1 | pound medium shrimp | 1/2 | cup mayonnaise |
| 1/3 | cup celery, chopped | 2 | teaspoons Old Bay seasoning |
| 2 | teaspoons fresh lemon juice | 1/4 | teaspoon Worcestershire |
| | | | sauce |

Cook, peel, and devein shrimp. Cut shrimp in half, and combine with remaining ingredients. Cover, and refrigerate 30 minutes or more. Stir before serving. Serve on sandwich roll, croissant, or bed of lettuce. Makes 4 servings.

# Sea Leg Salad

This light and refreshing salad is a family favorite when prepared by Gail, our daughter-in-law. She does everything well; this recipe is no exception. M.P.

| | |
|---|---|
| 1 8-ounce box Rainbow Trio macaroni | 1 pound sea legs (imitation crab meat) |
| 1 cup celery, chopped | 1/4 cup onion, diced |
| 1 cup mayonnaise | 2 Tablespoons vinegar |
| 1 teaspoon sugar salt and pepper | 1 cup green or red pepper, diced |

Boil macaroni, and drain. Combine mayonnaise, vinegar, sugar, salt, and pepper. In a large bowl, mix macaroni, mayonnaise mixture, and all other ingredients. Serve cold. (A 12-ounce box of macaroni will stretch the recipe without sacrificing flavor.) Serves 16.

*Gail Boyle Proffitt, Chesapeake, Virginia*

# Shrimp Potato Salad

| | |
|---|---|
| 4 cups potatoes, boiled | 1/4 cup olives, sliced |
| 3 hard-cooked eggs, chopped | 1 cup celery, chopped |
| 1/4 cup onion, chopped | 1/4 cup green pepper, chopped |
| 1/2 cup mayonnaise | 1/2 pound boiled shrimp, peeled |
| 1/2 teaspoon salt | |

Dice potatoes, and cut shrimp into salad-size pieces. Combine all ingredients, and mix well. Chill thoroughly before serving. Serves 8 to 10.

# Salmon Mousse

| | | | |
|---|---|---|---|
| 1 | envelope gelatin | 2 | Tablespoons lemon juice |
| 1 | small onion, sliced | 1/2 | cup boiling water |
| 1/2 | cup mayonnaise | 1/2 | teaspoon paprika |
| 1/2 | teaspoon dried dill | 1 | 1-pound can pink salmon |
| 1 | cup heavy cream | | |

In a blender, combine gelatin, lemon juice, onion, and boiling water. Blend until onion is just puréed. Add mayonnaise, paprika, dill, and salmon. Blend. Add cream, 1/3 cup at a time, and blend until smooth. Pour mixture into greased 1-quart mold, and chill several hours until firm. To unmold, dip bottom and sides into warm water, and turn onto a serving plate.

# Rice and Ham Salad

| | | | |
|---|---|---|---|
| 1 | 10-ounce package frozen green peas | 2 | cups cooked rice |
| 1 | Tablespoon onion, grated | 3/4 | cup mayonnaise |
| 1/2 | cup cooked ham, diced | 1/2 | cup dill pickle, diced |
| | dash paprika | 8 | ounces Cheddar cheese, cubed |
| | olives | | |

Cook peas, and drain. Gently combine mayonnaise, rice, onion, pickle, ham, and cheese. Fold in peas. Chill. Serve on a bed of lettuce leaves. Sprinkle with paprika; garnish with olives. Serves 8.

# Dressing for Cole Slaw

| | |
|---|---|
| 1 teaspoon prepared mustard | 2 Tablespoons sugar |
| 3 Tablespoons cream | 3 Tablespoons vinegar |
| pepper | paprika |
| celery seed | |

Mix all together then add vinegar last. Add other things if liked (apples, nuts, pepper, cukes, etc.) The cabbage should be crisp and cut very thin.

*Annie Harrell Stewart, Charlotte, North Carolina*

 # Cooked Salad Dressing

| | |
|---|---|
| 4 egg yolks | 2 teaspoons mustard |
| 3 Tablespoons sugar | 1 Tablespoon flour |
| 1 1/2 cups sweet milk | 3 Tablespoons butter |
| 1/2 cup vinegar | salt |
| cayenne pepper | |

Mix dry ingredients. Add beaten yolks, then butter melted, and let cool. Then milk and lastly vinegar. Cook in double boiler until nice and thick. Set aside to cool. You can make half this quantity if you like or you can double this.

*Annie Harrell Stewart, Charlotte, North Carolina*

 # Sugar Vinegar

To every gallon of spring water put two pounds of the very coarsest sugar; boil and skim thoroughly; then put one quart of cold water to every gallon of hot. When cool, put into it a toast spread with yeast. Stir it nine days; then barrel, and set it in a place where the sun will lie on it, with a bit of slate on the bunghole. Observe the caution about the barrel, as in gooseberry vinegar. Make in March; it will be ready in about six months.

# Soups, Stews and Sandwiches

## Mountain Cabin

*Family reunions held at the Proffitt cabin in the mountains
of Virginia enabled dozens of cousins to get to know each
other better and love each other more. — M.P.*

# SOUPS, STEWS, AND SANDWICHES
## Soups

### Beef and Vegetable Soup

beef, sirloin or T-bone
onion, as desired, chopped
1 can mixed vegetables, drained
1 can shoe peg corn, drained

1 can tomatoes
1 can tomato and okra, drained
1 or 2 cans tomato soup
handful of rice

Cut meat from bone and fat. Put in big, heavy pot (use bone and as much of the fat as you wish). Add 1 can tomatoes, and onion. Add lots of water (1/2 potful). Cook about 1 1/2 to 2 hours slowly. Add 1 can tomatoes and okra, 1 can mixed vegetables, tomato soup (undiluted), 1 can shoe peg corn, and some rice. Cook slowly a long time. Remove bone and fat. Refrigerate soup. Later skim fat off. (The tomato soup makes the difference!)

*Mary S. Moss, Washington, North Carolina*

### Curry Soup

8 ounces cream cheese,
softened
1 teaspoon curry powder

2 cans consommé, room
temperature
parsley

In a blender, mix cheese, curry powder, and half a can of the consomme. Pour into 8 serving cups. Cover, and chill overnight. Carefully spoon rest of consomme into the chilled cups. Chill another 6 to 8 hours. Garnish with parsley.

# Cabbage Soup with Meat Balls

|  |  |  |  |
|---|---|---|---|
| 2 | heads hard cabbage, shredded | 1 | large can tomato juice |
|  |  | 1 | large can water |
| 2 or 3 | carrots, grated | 2 or 3 | stalks celery, chopped |
| 1 | package dried vegetables | 1 | large onion, chopped |
| 1 | large spoon lemon juice | 1 | large spoon artificial |
|  | salt |  | sweetener or less |

Combine ingredients, and stew 1 to 1 1/2 hours.

**Meatballs:**

|  |  |  |  |
|---|---|---|---|
| 1 | to 1 1/2 pounds ground beef or veal | 1 | egg, slightly beaten |
|  |  | 1/2 | cup quick cooking rice |
| 1 | small onion, chopped |  | salt and pepper to taste |

Combine ingredients, and form into balls. Drop into soup mixture. Cook until meatballs are done.

*Janie Proffitt Flippo, Roanoke, Virginia*

# Carrot Soup

|  |  |  |  |
|---|---|---|---|
| 2 | cups carrots, chopped | 1 | can chicken broth |
| 1/4 | teaspoon thyme | 1/4 | teaspoon nutmeg |
| 2 | Tablespoons butter | 3 | Tablespoons flour |
| 1 | cup milk |  |  |

Cook carrots with chicken broth and seasonings until tender, about 10 minutes. Put in blender and blend until smooth. Melt butter; add flour. Stir, and cook 1 minute. Stir in milk, and cook until thickened, stirring constantly. Stir in carrot mixture. Serve hot or cold.

# Calico Bean Soup

I received this recipe, along with the colorful mixture of beans needed to prepare it, from one of the staff members of a high school in Virginia Beach where I happily served as librarian for several years. I thought it was a great holiday gift idea.  M.P.

| | |
|---|---|
| 2 ounces kidney beans | 2 ounces navy beans |
| 2 ounces black-eyed peas | 2 ounces barley |
| 2 ounces lentils | 1 ounces split peas |
| 2 ounces northern beans | 1 large onion chopped |
| 1 large can tomatoes | 1 teaspoon garlic powder |
| juice of 1 lemon | salt and pepper to taste |
| water | 1 pound ham, diced |

Wash beans, place in a large kettle, and cover with water.  Add 2 tablespoons of salt. Soak overnight.  In the morning, drain, and add 2 quarts of water and ham.  Simmer 2 to 3 hours; then add other ingredients.  Simmer another 30 minutes or so.  Serve with bread or crackers and a salad.

*Kempsville High School, Virginia Beach, Virginia*

 # Colorings for Soups and Gravies

Put four ounces of lump sugar, a gill of water, and half an ounce of the finest butter into a small tosser, and set it over a gentle fire.  Stir it with a wooden spoon until it becomes a bright brown.  Then add half a pint of water; boil, skim, and, when cold, bottle and cork it tight.  Add to soup or gravy as much of this as will give a proper color.

# Corn Soup

| | | | | |
|---|---|---|---|---|
| 6 | ears corn | 4 | quarts water |
| | salt and pepper | 3 | Tablespoons butter |
| 2 | Tablespoons flour | 1 | pint milk or cream |
| 2 | egg yolks, beaten | | |

Scrape the corn from the cob. Place the scraped cobs into 4 quarts of boiling water, and cook until about three quarts of water remain. Remove cobs, and replace with corn. Cook for another 1/2 hour or until corn is soft enough to be pressed through a sieve. After straining corn, season liberally with salt and pepper. Rub the flour into the butter, and add to soup. When mixture begins to thicken, add the boiling cream, stirring constantly. Cook a few minutes more, and remove from heat. Mix in beaten egg yolks. They give the finishing touch to a delicious soup.

# Split Pea Soup

My husband does much of the daily cooking at our house. He loves to cook, and I love to let him. He makes many delicious foods, but I think soups are his specialty. M.P.

| | | | |
|---|---|---|---|
| 1 | pound package dry split peas | 1/2 | pound smoked ham, |
| 1/2 | large onion, diced | | finely diced |
| 1/2 | teaspoon garlic powder | 2 | bay leaves |
| 1/2 | teaspoon pepper | 8 to 10 | cups water |
| | salt to taste | | |

Rinse peas thoroughly before placing in a large, heavy pot. Cover with water. Add ham, onion, garlic powder, pepper, and bay leaves. Bring to a heavy boil, and cook two minutes. Reduce heat to simmer. Cover; let cook 2 to 3 hours or even longer if you like. Add salt to taste during the last thirty minutes. Add more pepper if desired. Remove bay leaves before serving.

*Don Proffitt, Virginia Beach, Virginia*

# French Onion Soup

| | | | |
|---|---|---|---|
| 3 | medium onions, sliced | 4 | cups boiling water |
| | French bread, not fresh | | Swiss cheese, imported |
| | butter | | grated |
| | ovenproof cookware | | |

Saute onions in butter in frying pan. Add water to the onions, and let simmer about 10 minutes. Break or cut bread, and place in bottom of ovenproof soup bowls. Pour soup from frying pan on top of the bread. Spread a generous amount of cheese on top of soup. Place in preheated oven that has been set on broil. Broil about 10 minutes.

*Jeannine Moss, Winston-Salem, North Carolina*

# Mother's Quick Potato Soup

This was one of my favorites when I was growing up. It still is. I am not sure that this is precisely my mother's recipe, but it's the way I make it, and it suits me — and my family. M.P.

| | | | |
|---|---|---|---|
| 2 or 3 | slices bacon | 1 | medium onion, chopped |
| 4 | medium potatoes, diced | 1 | cup potato stock |
| 2 | cups milk | | fresh parsley, or flakes |
| | salt | | pepper |

Dice potatoes, and cook in salted water until nearly done. Reserve 1 cup of the stock. While potatoes are cooking, cut bacon into small pieces; fry until crisp but not hard. Drain most of fat from pan. Add chopped onion, and cook until slightly browned. Transfer bacon and onions into soup-sized pot. Add potatoes, potato stock, milk, parsley, salt and pepper to taste. Cook over low heat about 20 minutes or until potatoes finish cooking and flavors meld.

*Alice Heath Taylor, Norfolk, Virginia*

# Tomato Soup

| | |
|---|---|
| 1   quart ripe tomatoes | 1   quart water |
| 1   teaspoon salt | 1   teaspoon pepper |
| 1   teaspoon sugar | 1/4   stick butter |
| 1   quart milk | |

Boil tomatoes in water for 10 minutes. Add salt, pepper, sugar, and butter. Stir until butter is melted. Gradually stir in milk; simmer until thoroughly heated and flavors blend.

# Vegetable Soup

| | |
|---|---|
| 1 1/2   pounds lean stew beef | 1   large onion, chopped |
| 2   stalks celery, chopped | 2   Tablespoons oil or less |
| large amount cold water | corn |
| lima beans | green beans |
| peas | carrots |
| cabbage | 4   white potatoes, diced |
| 2   cans tomatoes, diced | salt |
| pepper | 2   bay leaves |
| 1   Tablespoon parsley flakes | |

Cut beef into bite-size pieces. In a large, heavy pot, brown beef in oil. Add cold water; put in onion, celery, and bay leaves. Cover; simmer for 2 hours. Except for tomatoes and potatoes, add vegetables plus salt and pepper to taste. Cook another hour. The potatoes, tomatoes, and parsley flakes should then be added along with more salt and pepper if needed. Cook another 30 minutes. Remove bay leaves before serving. Fresh or canned vegetables may be used. Leave out the ones you don't like. Of course, you know this soup will taste better the day after cooking.

*Margaret Taylor Proffitt, Virginia Beach, Virginia*

# Stews

## Beef Stew

| | |
|---|---|
| 2 1/2 pounds lean beef | 4 beef boullion cubes |
| 1 large bay leaf | 2 teaspoons salt |
| 1/4 teaspoon pepper | 1/8 teaspoon oregano |
| 1/4 teaspoon parsley flakes | 1/8 teaspoon rosemary |
| 1/8 teaspoon thyme | 1 medium green pepper, finely |
| 1 medium onion, thinly sliced | chopped |
| 6 carrots, cut in bite-sized | 6 medium potatoes, cubed |
| pieces | 3/4 cup flour |
| 1 quart water | |

Bring water to boil in a heavy pot. Dissolve beef cubes in another 2 cups of boiling water, and add this to the boiling water in the heavy pot. In a skillet, sear beef in its own fat. A little oil may be added if needed. Put beef into the pot, and add salt, pepper, herbs, green pepper, and onion. Simmer for 2 hours; then add carrots and potatoes. Simmer 1 additional hour. During the last 30 minutes, add the 3/4 cup of flour which has been mixed with enough water to make a smooth paste.

*Mary S. Moss, Washington, North Carolina*

## Fish Stew

Cut 2 pounds of Rock fish into serving size pieces. Place slices of onion in bottom of greased pot; add a layer of sliced white potatoes and a layer of fish. Add 1 teaspoon Worcestershire sauce and 4 medium cans of V-8 juice. Cook until potatoes are tender and fish is done. Add small corn dumplings the last 15 minutes of cooking time, or baked cornbread may be served instead.

# Brunswick Stew

Many recipes I picked up during my teaching career make the memories of the friendships I formed even more dear. This one came from one of the nicest people I ever worked with. The narrative is hers. M.P.

"My early memories of Brunswick stew was watching with interest as the stew was cooked outdoors in an iron stew pot over live coals. This version of the stew substituted chicken and pork (fat back) for the gamier ingredients. Simmering the meat until it has separated from the bone blends flavors and creates the proper full-bodied taste and mushy texture.

"Only fresh vegetables from our garden were added to the pot after the meats were tender and removed from the bone. This mixture was then cooked for hours and hours, until a consistency (thick and yummy) was obtained. And, by the way, this was a watched pot — stirred at intervals to prevent sticking. My version, much simplified, follows:

| | | | |
|---|---|---|---|
| 1 | large hen, cut up | 2 | large onions, sliced |
| 2 | cans lima beans | 2 | cans tomatoes, diced |
| 2 | cans corn | 3 | medium potatoes, diced |
| 3 | teaspoons salt | 1 | teaspoon black pepper |
| 1 | Tablespoon sugar | | water |
| | bay leaves | | |

"Cook chicken, with enough water to cover, until tender. Reserve 1 quart of liquid for thick stew, or 2 quarts for thin stew. Remove chicken from bones and dice into bite-size pieces. Put vegetables into boiling stew and add chicken. Simmer on low heat until desired consistency is obtained. Stir frequently to avoid sticking. Add several bay leaves to cooked mixture and refrigerate. Heat only the amount you plan to serve as it keeps several days." (Note: 4 cups of fresh lima beans, tomatoes, and corn may be substituted for canned.)

*Louise Bland, Kitty Hawk, North Carolina*

# Oyster Stew

| | | | | |
|---|---|---|---|---|
| 1/4 | cup all-purpose flour | | 1/4 | cup water |
| 4 | teaspoons salt | | 4 | teaspoons Worcestershire |
| 2 | 8-ounce containers | | | sauce |
| | shucked oysters | | 8 | cups half and half |
| 3 | Tablespoons butter | | 3 | Tablespoons chopped |
| | or margarine | | | parsley |

In a 4-quart pan, combine flour, water, salt, and Worcestershire sauce. Add oysters, along with their liquid. Cook over a medium to low heat for 10 to 15 minutes until oysters curl and centers are firm. Add butter and half and half. Gradually heat to boiling. Remove from heat, and let stand 10 minutes. Garnish with parsley. 10 cups or 6 main dish servings.

# Jim's Clam Chowder

Our children and many of our friends always look forward to Jim's clam chowder. If you like the taste of clams, you will love this chowder. One cup or bowl won't be enough! M.D.

| | | | | |
|---|---|---|---|---|
| 4 | pints clams, with juice | | 1 | large stalk celery |
| 8 | medium potatoes | | 2 | large onions |
| 2 | Tablespoons butter | | | |

Chop up the clams, celery, potatoes, and onion. Put in large pot with clam juice and water (pot about 3/4 full), and bring to a boil. Reduce heat. Let simmer, covered, until potatoes, onions, and celery have cooked. Makes approximately 6 quarts. Optional: To reduce the clam flavor, you can cook a strip of bacon in the pot before adding the other ingredients. You can also add carrots (chopped) and a can of tomatoes.

*Jim Darden, Virginia Beach, Virginia*

# Sandwiches

## Chicken and Pineapple Sandwiches

1   8-ounce can crushed
pineapple, drained
2   cups walnuts, chopped
24  slices white bread, buttered

1   cup cooked chicken,
chopped
1/2 cup cooked salad dressing

Combine pineapple, chicken, nuts, and salad dressing.  Spread on buttered
bread.  For party sandwiches, remove crust from bread, and cut diagonally into
quarters.  (See index for cooked salad dressing recipe.)

## Pimento Cheese Sandwich Spread

Pimento cheese was always an essential food item during the week we spent
with my parents at the beach in North Carolina.  My sister, Sara, and I would
eat pimento cheese sandwiches and pimento cheese on crackers.  In fact,
Mother, Sara, and I would usually have a container of pimento cheese and a
box of crackers next to us!  M.D.

1   10-ounce package yellow, extra
sharp Cracker Barrel Cheese
3   Tablespoons mayonnaise
Worcestershire sauce
1   small onion, grated

1   package white or sharp
cheese
2   7-ounce jars pimentos, diced
or sliced, with juice

Grate cheeses, and combine with other ingredients.  Refrigerate in closed
container.

*Sara Moss McCowen, Richmond, Virginia*

# Cheese for Sandwiches

| | | | |
|---|---|---|---|
| 1 | pound cheese, grated | 1 | tall can Carnation milk |
| | salt | | red pepper |
| | onion juice | | |

Heat cheese and milk in top of a double boiler until blended and thickened. Add salt, red pepper, and onion juice to taste. Refrigerate. Serve as sandwich spread or with crackers.

*Mary S. Moss, Washington, North Carolina*

# Walnut Tuna Sandwiches

| | | | |
|---|---|---|---|
| 1 | 7-ounce can white tuna | 1/2 | cup walnuts, finely chopped |
| 2 | Tablespoons sweet pickles, finely chopped | 1 | Tablespoon green pepper, finely chopped |
| 1 | Tablespoon pimento, finely chopped | 1/2 | teaspoon salt |
| 20 | slices bread, buttered | 6 to 8 | Tablespoons mayonnaise |

Flake tuna. Add remaining ingredients, except bread, and blend well. Spread on slices of buttered bread. Makes 10 sandwiches. Crusts may be cut from bread for party occasions.

# Smithfield Ham Spread

| | | | |
|---|---|---|---|
| 1/2 | pound Smithfield ham, ground | 1/2 | cup mayonnaise |
| 2 | Tablespoons mustard | 2 | Tablespoons butter, softened |

*Mary S. Moss Washington, North Carolina*

# Fish Sandwiches

| | | | | |
|---|---|---|---|---|
| 2 | eggs, hard boiled | 6 | frozen fish fillets |
| 3 | Tablespoons butter or margarine | 3 | Tablespoons flour |
| | | 3/4 | teaspoon curry powder |
| 3/4 | teaspoon dry mustard | 2 1/4 | cups milk |
| 1 | teaspoon minced onion | 1 | cup cheese, cubed |
| 1 | Tablespoon lemon juice | 6 | sandwich buns |
| | salt | | pepper |

Toast buns under broiler; remove and spread with butter.  Broil fish until done.
In a saucepan, melt butter.  Stir in dry ingredients.  Add milk and onion.  Cook
and stir until mixture thickens.  Add cheese; stir until melted.  Chop hard
boiled eggs and add to sauce.  Sprinkle fish with lemon juice.  Use sauce as
dressing for sandwiches.

# Deviled Eggs for Sandwiches

| | | | | |
|---|---|---|---|---|
| 6 | hard boiled eggs, chopped | 1 | cup sweet pickle relish |
| 1 | teaspoon sugar | 1/2 | teaspoon salt |
| 1/2 | Tablespoon mustard | 1/2 | teaspoon celery seed |
| 3 | Tablespoons mayonnaise | | |

Combine and mix well.

# Ham Sandwich Spread

Grind 1/2 pound of cooked ham, 1 sweet pickle, and 4 hard cooked eggs.
Season with salt, pepper, and prepared mustard.  Moisten with vinegar until it
is the right consistency to spread.

# Sweets

## Lynnhaven Elementary School

*Lynnhaven Elementary School opened in September 1963
in Virginia Beach. Over the years the school has seen many
changes, including the addition of kindergarten classes,
increased staff, additional classrooms, and a gymnasium.
— M.D.*

# SWEETS

## Cakes

## Anne's Chocolate Cake

This delicious cake was first shared with me when Anne and I worked together several years ago. We became friends, and she would sometimes make the cake for my birthday. All of us in the First Colonial High library would have invented an occasion, if necessary, to have Anne's chocolate cake.   M.D.

| | |
|---|---|
| 1   package fudge cake mix | 2   eggs, beaten |
| 1   teaspoon almond extract | 1   can cherry pie filling |

Combine cake mix, eggs, and flavoring. Stir by hand until well mixed. Blend in pie filling. Grease bottom of 9x13-inch pan with solid shortening or margarine. Bake in 350 degree oven for 25 to 30 minutes or until toothpick comes out clean.

### Frosting:

| | |
|---|---|
| 1   cup sugar | 5   Tablespoons butter |
| 1/3   cup milk |      or margarine |
| 1   6-ounce package semi-sweet       chocolate chips | |

Prepare frosting while cake is baking. In a small saucepan, combine sugar, butter, and milk. Boil 1 minute, stirring constantly. Remove from heat, and stir in chocolate chips until smooth. Pour over partially cooled cake.

*Anne Hopewell, Virginia Beach, Virginia*

# Our Emily's Chocolate Cake

Early morning visits by faculty members to Mama Groover's kitchen at Lynnhaven Elementary School would most often result in a specially prepared snack meant to get the day's teaching off to a good start. The delicious sticky buns, donuts, or brownies were much appreciated treats prepared by Mama Groover and her staff. These coffee snacks also provided us with the first aromas of wonderful chocolate cake being baked as dessert for the lunchtime meal. That cake is still talked about in glowing terms whenever former faculty members or students get together to reminisce. As far as we know, no one has successfully reduced the ingredients to make a family size cake, but we think it is interesting to see the huge amounts needed to make enough cake for a school full of children. M. & M.

| | | | |
|---|---|---|---|
| 17 1/2 | pounds flour | 17 | pounds sugar |
| 28 | ounces Hershey's cocoa | 1 | heaping cup baking soda |
| 6 1/2 | Tablespoons salt | 1 | gallon oil |
| 2 1/2 | cups vinegar | 6 | ounces vanilla |
| 2 1/2 | gallons cold water | | |

Mix dry ingredients together in cafeteria size mixer. Make 3 wells. Pour oil in the first well, vinegar in the second, and vanilla in the third. While these ingredients are mixing, pour the cold water over all until the batter is well-blended. Pour into 7 greased 18x26-inch sheet cake pans. Bake at 350 degrees. Spread frosting while cake is warm.

**Frosting:**

| | | | |
|---|---|---|---|
| 42 | ounces butter | 14 | pounds confectioners' sugar |
| 7 | cups cocoa | 1 1/2 | teaspoons salt |
| 4 1/2 | cups boiling water | 7 | tablespoons vanilla |

Cream butter. Combine dry ingredients; mix with butter. Stir in boiling water. Blend in vanilla. Mix frosting until smooth, and spread on warm cake.

# Chocolate Cake

| | |
|---|---|
| 2 squares chocolate | 2 Tablespoons butter |
| 1 1/2 cups flour | 1 cup sugar |
| 1 teaspoon soda | 1 egg yolk, slightly beaten |
| 1 cup milk | 1 teaspoon vanilla |

Melt the chocolate and butter together. Sift flour, sugar, and soda together. Combine slightly beaten egg yolk and milk. Add dry ingredients to egg mixture, and beat with egg beater. Add chocolate mixture and vanilla. Blend well. Pour into shallow pan. Place in cold oven. Bake for 45 minutes at 350 degrees. Do not open oven door during first 20 minutes of baking.

**White Caramel Icing:**

| | |
|---|---|
| 1 cup granulated sugar | 1/2 cup milk, scant |
| butter the size of a walnut | |

Combine ingredients, and bring to a boil. Boil until stringy. Test just like brown sugar icing.

*Annie Harrell Stewart, Charlotte, North Carolina*

# Granny's Chocolate Cake

One small cup of butter, one cup of sweet milk, 2 cups of sugar, three and one-half cups of flour, four eggs, three teaspoonfuls of baking powder. *Chocolate for cake:* Six tablespoonfuls of bakers' chocolate, grated fine; scald with milk enough to make a paste to spread easily, and flavor with vanilla.

# Mary's Chocolate Cake

| | |
|---|---|
| 1/2 teaspoon salt | 2 cups sugar |
| 2 cups flour | 4 Tablespoons cocoa |
| 2 sticks margarine | 1 cup water |
| 2 eggs | 1 teaspoon vanilla |
| 1 teaspoon soda | 1/2 cup buttermilk |

Preheat oven. Sift flour, salt, and sugar into a large mixing bowl. Combine cocoa, margarine, and water. Cook for a few minutes after margarine melts. Pour hot cocoa mixture into dry mixture. Stir well. Add eggs and mix; then add vanilla. Lastly, add buttermilk that has been mixed with the soda. Pour into greased 11 1/2x16-inch pan and bake in 400 degree oven for 20 minutes. Frost with a chocolate icing.

*Mary S. Moss, Washington, North Carolina*

# Chocolate Chip Date Cake

| | |
|---|---|
| 1 cup boiling water | 1 cup dates, chopped |
| 1 teaspoon baking soda | 1 cup shortening |
| 1 cup sugar | 2 eggs, beaten |
| 1 3/4 cups flour | 2 Tablespoons cocoa |
| 1/4 teaspoon salt | 1 6-ounce package |
| 1/2 cup nuts, chopped | chocolate chips |

Combine water, dates, and baking soda. Cream shortening and sugar; add beaten eggs, flour, cocoa, salt, and date mixture. Mix well. Pour into 9x13-inch greased pan. Sprinkle with chocolate chips and nuts. Bake at 350 degrees for 30 minutes. Sprinkle with powdered sugar if desired.

# Chocolate Chip Cake

| | | | |
|---|---|---|---|
| 1 | box yellow cake mix | 1 | box instant vanilla pudding |
| 1/2 | cup vegetable oil | 4 | eggs |
| 1 | cup milk | 1 | bar sweet German chocolate, |
| 1 | 6-ounce package chocolate | | grated |
| | chips | | |

Reserve 1/4 cup of the grated chocolate. Mix all ingredients. Bake in bundt or tube pan in a 350 degree oven for 50 to 55 minutes. Remove from pan, and let cool.

**Glaze:**

| | | | |
|---|---|---|---|
| 1 | cup powdered sugar | 4 | Tablespoons milk |
| 1/4 | cup powdered sugar | | reserved chocolate shavings |

When cake has cooled, mix the cup of powdered sugar with the milk. Glaze cake with mixture. Dredge reserved chocolate shavings in the powdered sugar, and sprinkle over cake.

# Chocolate Truffle Cake

| | | | |
|---|---|---|---|
| 2/3 | cup butter | 1 | 12-ounce package |
| 1 1/2 | teaspoons flour | | chocolate chips |
| 1 1/2 | teaspoons sugar | 1/4 | teaspoon salt |
| 4 | eggs, separated | | whipped topping |

Melt butter and chips in top of double boiler. Add flour, sugar, and salt, and stir thoroughly. Beat in egg yolks, one at a time. Beat whites until stiff, then fold into yolk mixture. Pour into a deep, greased, floured, 8-inch cake or springform pan. Bake at 325 degrees about 40 minutes until tester comes out clean. Cool 15 minutes before cutting. Top with whipped topping.

# Mississippi Mud Cake

| | |
|---|---|
| 2 cups flour | 2 cups sugar |
| 1/2 teaspoon salt | 1 teaspoon cinnamon |
| 2 sticks butter or use half butter and half shortening | 1 cup water |
| | 3 Tablespoons cocoa |
| 2 eggs, beaten | 1 teaspoon soda |
| 1/2 cup buttermilk | 1 teaspoon vanilla |

Sift flour, sugar, salt, and cinnamon together. Bring butter, water, and cocoa to a boil, and pour over the flour mixture. Mix eggs, soda, buttermilk, and vanilla. Combine all mixtures, and blend well. Pour into a greased 9x13x2-inch pan. Bake in a 350 degree oven for 20 minutes.

**Icing:**

| | |
|---|---|
| 1 stick butter or margarine | 3 Tablespoons cocoa |
| 6 Tablespoons milk | 1 box confectioners' sugar |
| 1/2 cup pecans, chopped | 1 teaspoon vanilla |

Mix butter, cocoa, and milk. Heat, and mix with pecans, sugar, and vanilla. Frost cake immediately.

 # Chocolate Nut Cake

One cup of butter, two cups of sugar, three eggs, four-fifths of a cup of milk, three cups of flour. *Paste:* two ounces of grated chocolate, one-half cup of milk, one cup of sugar, and one-half cup of nuts.

# Chocolate Pound Cake

| | |
|---|---|
| 1/2 cup butter or margarine | 1/2 cup shortening |
| 3 cups sugar | 5 eggs |
| 3 cups flour | 1/4 teaspoon baking powder |
| 1/2 cup cocoa | 1 1/4 cups milk |
| 1 teaspoon vanilla | |

Cream together butter and shortening. Add sugar, and mix well. Beat in eggs one at a time. Sift dry ingredients together. Alternately add the dry ingredients and the milk to the creamed mixture. Blend in vanilla. Bake in greased and floured tube pan in a 325 degree oven for 1 hour and 30 minutes.

**Icing:**

| | |
|---|---|
| 2 cups sugar | 1 stick butter |
| 2 squares chocolate | 2/3 cup evaporated milk |
| 1 teaspoon vanilla | |

Combine all ingredients. Bring to boil, and cook for 2 minutes. Cool, and beat until stiff enough to spread.

*Janie Proffitt Flippo, Roanoke, Virginia*

# Romeo and Juliet Cake

*Juliet* — One cup of white sugar, whites of six eggs, well beaten; one table-spoonful of butter, one and one-half cups of flour, one heaping teaspoonful of baking powder, four tablespoonfuls of sweet milk. *Romeo* — One cup of sugar, one tablespoonful of butter, yokes of six eggs, one cup of flour, four tablespoonfuls of sweet milk, one heaping teaspoonful of baking powder. Bake in separate tins. Beat the whites of two eggs to a stiff froth, add the grated rind and juice of lemon; thicken this with pulverized sugar, and spread between the cakes.

# Apple Pecan Cake

3 eggs, beaten
2 cups sugar
1 teaspoon salt
2 teaspoons vanilla
1 cup pecans, chopped.

1 1/2 cups salad oil
3 cups flour
1 teaspoon baking soda
3 cups raw apples, finely chopped

Mix eggs, salad oil, and sugar. In a separate bowl, sift together flour, salt, and baking soda. Add to the egg mixture; then add vanilla, apples, and pecans. Bake in a 13x9-inch pan in a 350 degree oven for 45 minutes. Cool before adding topping.

**Topping:**
1 stick margarine
1/4 cup evaporated milk

1 cup brown sugar
whipped cream (optional)

Melt margarine, and add brown sugar and milk. Cook to a rolling boil. Continue boiling for 2 or 3 minutes, stirring constantly. Makes about 16 servings. Squares can be topped with a nice dollop of whipped cream.

 # Mrs. Burnham's Fig Cake

One cup of sugar, one cup of flour, half a cup of butter, half a cup of sweet milk, half a cup of cornstarch, two teaspoonfuls of baking powder mixed in flour, whites of four eggs, well whipped and stirred in last. Bake the cake in round tins for layers.

*Filling:*
Three-fourths of a pound of figs, chopped fine, one cup of sugar in five tablespoonfuls of hot water. Bring to a boil and turn over the figs. When cooled spread between the layers of the cake. Makes three layers of cake and two of figs.

# Dr. Byrd Cake

We have found several versions of this cake, variously called The Humming-bird Cake, the Jamaican Doctor Bird Cake, Dr. Byrd's Pound Cake, and the Dr. Byrd Cake. Some recipes leave out the coconut, substituting the pineapple. Some, as ours does, include both. Our research tells us that the doctor bird is the national bird of Jamaica. It seems fitting that finding bananas in such abundance on their island, the Jamaicans would create this wonderful combination of ingredients. M. & M.

| | | | |
|---|---|---|---|
| 3 | cups plain flour | 2 | cups sugar |
| 1 | teaspoon soda | 1 | teaspoon cinnamon |
| 1 | teaspoon salt | 1 1/2 | cups oil |
| 1 1/2 | teaspoons vanilla | 3 | eggs |
| 2 | cups mashed bananas | 1 | 3-ounce package coconut |
| 1 | cup chopped nuts | 1 | 4 ounce can crushed pineapple, undrained |

Mix oil and sugar. Beat eggs, and add to oil mixture. Sift dry ingredients and combine with oil and egg mixture. Add vanilla and nuts. Stir in bananas, coconut, and pineapple. Bake 1 hour at 350 degrees in a bundt pan, a tube pan, or 2 loaf pans. Cool cake before icing.

**Icing:** (Optional)

| | | | |
|---|---|---|---|
| 1/2 | cup whipped margarine, not stick | 1 | 8-ounce package cream cheese |
| 1 | teaspoon vanilla extract | 16 | ounces confectioners' sugar, sifted |

Soften margarine and cream cheese. Add vanilla, and mix with a spoon. Work in small amounts of sugar at a time. Icing will naturally be stiff. Do not use an electric mixer.

# Lemon Poppy Seed Cake

| | |
|---|---|
| 1 package yellow cake mix | 1/2 cup sugar |
| 1/3 cup vegetable oil | 1/4 cup water |
| 1 cup plain nonfat yogurt | 1 cup egg substitute |
| 3 Tablespoons lemon juice | 2 Tablespoons poppy seeds |
| cooking spray | lemon glaze |

In a large mixing bowl, combine cake mix and sugar. Add oil, water, yogurt, lemon juice, and egg substitute. Beat at medium speed for 6 minutes. Stir in poppy seeds. Pour batter in large bundt pan that has been sprayed with cooking spray. Bake in 350 degree oven for about 40 minutes or until toothpick comes out clean. Cool in pan on wire rack. Remove from pan, drizzle with lemon glaze, and finish cooling process on wire rack.

**Glaze:**
Combine 1/2 cup sifted powdered sugar and 2 tablespoons lemon juice. Stir until smooth. Drizzle over cake.

# Perfect Pound Cake

| | |
|---|---|
| 2 cups sugar | 1/2 pound butter |
| 5 eggs | 3 cups sifted flour |
| 1 can evaporated milk | 1 teaspoon baking powder |
| 1/2 teaspoon salt | 1 1/2 teaspoons vanilla |

Preheat oven to 300 degrees. Cream butter. Add a little sugar, a little flour, and a little milk; then add 1 egg. Repeat until you have used all the sugar, eggs, and flour, and 1/2 cup of the milk. Add flavoring. Beat baking powder into the remaining 1/2 cup milk, and add to batter. Pour into well-greased tube pan. Bake 1 1/2 hours in preheated 300 degree oven.

*Annie Harrell Stewart, Charlotte, North Carolina*

## Sour Cream Coconut Cake

When my husband worked at the central office of the Virginia Beach School System, any special occasion would bring a request for this delicious cake. He had collected the recipe some years earlier, and he makes it like no one else can. Yummmmmm! M.P.

| | | | |
|---|---|---|---|
| 1 | butter yellow cake mix | 2 | cups sugar |
| 2 | cups sour cream | 18 | ounces frozen coconut |

Mix cake as directed. Bake in 2 round cake pans. When cool, split into 4 layers. Mix sugar, sour cream, and coconut. Spread on each layer and over top and sides of cake. Store in airtight container in refrigerator for 3 to 5 days before serving.

*Jane Cheek, Virginia Beach, Virginia*

 ## Wedding Cake

Long ago, my mother told me that the wedding cakes she remembered from her childhood were not the multilayered, white-iced, beauties of today, but were more like fruit cakes. This recipe for wedding cake seems to confirm her recollection. M. P.

Six cups of butter, three pints of sugar, six pounds of raisins, six pounds of currants, two pounds of citron, two pounds of shelled almonds, one pint of brandy, one tablespoonful of all kinds of spices, twenty eggs, three quarts of browned flour; beat the butter and sugar together; add the spices, fruits, nuts and brandy; then add your eggs, well beaten, and the browned flour sifted. This quantity will make three large loaves, and will keep for years. Bake in a moderate oven four hours.

# Hermit Cake

This recipe was given to us by my husband's mother. She cooked and baked everything well. This hermit cake, though more popular recently, used to be rare and was often substituted at Christmastime for fruit cake. My husband is the hermit cake baker in our household and still considers this a holiday cake. Although he doesn't bake them every year, we all enjoy them when he does. He and his sister compare notes about how their Hermit Cakes turn out.   M.P.

| | |
|---|---|
| 1   pound butter | 1 1/2   pounds brown sugar |
| 6   eggs | 6   cups flour |
| 2   scant Tablespoons lemon extract, or juice and grated peel of 1 lemon | 2   Tablespoons vanilla |
| | 1   Tablespoon cinnamon |
| | 1   pound walnuts, chopped |
| 1/2   cup pecans, chopped | 2   pound dates, chopped |
| 1   teaspoon baking powder | sliced apples |
| apple wine | |

Reserve a few walnut halves. Dredge fruit in 1/4 cup flour; set aside. (If you wish, you may omit some of the dates and use raisins instead.) Cream butter and sugar. Add eggs, and beat well. Sift flour, cinnamon, and baking powder together; add lemon juice; then add vanilla. Mix well; add fruit and nuts, and mix well again. Batter will be very stiff. Spoon and scrape into 2 greased and floured tube pans. Place reserved walnut halves on top of batter to decorate cakes. Bake in a 275 degree oven for 2 1/2 hours. Place a pan of hot water on the lower shelf of the oven while cakes are baking. Place sliced apples on top of cakes after they have cooled. Dampen (do not wet) a paper towel or cloth with apple wine, and drape over top and sides of cake. Store in covered tin. Cloth may need to be dampened from time to time during storage. Keep in a cool place. Baking the cakes 2 weeks ahead of the holidays allows time for the apple and wine flavors to combine with the flavors in the cake.

*Mae Hogan Proffitt, Roanoke, Virginia*

# Washington and Domestic Cake

Two pounds of sugar, one and one-half pounds of butter, four and one-half pounds of flour, one and one-half pounds of lard, five eggs, one pint of milk, half an ounce of ammonia, and mace. (Comment: Fat City!)

## Janie's Lemon Pound Cake

| | | | |
|---|---|---|---|
| 3 | cups sugar | 3 | cups flour (sifted) |
| 6 | eggs | 1 | teaspoon baking powder |
| 1 | cup milk | 2 | sticks margarine |
| 1/2 | cup Crisco shortening | 2 | Tablespoons lemon extract |
| 1 | teaspoon vanilla | | |

Cream sugar, margarine, and shortening until very smooth. Add eggs, and beat well. Combine baking powder with sifted flour. Add flour mixture to creamy mixture alternately with milk. Stir in lemon and vanilla flavorings. Bake at 350 degrees for 1 hour 20 minutes. Do not open oven door while baking, as the cake falls easily. Add glaze while cake is still warm.

**Glaze:**

    2  cups confectioners' sugar       1/2  cup Real Lemon

While cake is warm, dribble top with spoonfuls of glaze. Dip a paper towel in remaining glaze and pat sides of cake. Store in airtight container.

*Janie Proffitt Flippo, Roanoke, Virginia*

133

# Kentucky Pound Cake

| | |
|---|---|
| 2 1/2 cups self-rising flour | 2 cups sugar |
| 1 1/4 cups vegetable oil | 1 cup crushed pineapple |
| 4 eggs, separated | 2 Tablespoons hot water |
| 1 1/2 teaspoons cinnamon | 2 cups chopped pecans |
| 1 cup black walnuts | |

Preheat oven to 350 degrees. First beat egg whites, and set aside. Drain pineapple, and save juice for glaze. Beat flour, sugar, salad oil, and pineapple. Add egg yolks, cinnamon, and hot water. Fold nuts into beaten egg whites. Fold this into cake mixture at low speed. Pour into prepared tube pan, and bake at 350 degrees for 1 hour 10 minutes. Keeps well and also can be frozen.

**Glaze:**

| | |
|---|---|
| 1 cup powdered sugar | pineapple juice |

Mix sugar and enough pineapple juice to make glaze of proper consistency to drizzle over top of cake.

*Dottie Reynolds, Louisa, Virginia*

# Old-Fashioned Pound Cake

| | |
|---|---|
| 1 pound butter | 1 pound sugar |
| 1 pound flour (3 1/4 cups) | 10 eggs, separated |
| 1/4 teaspoon mace or nutmeg | 2 Tablespoons brandy |

Cream butter well, and gradually add the sugar, beating after each addition. Beat the egg yolks until thick and lemon colored, and add to butter and sugar mixture. Stir in brandy. Sift the flour and mace or nutmeg, and add alternately with the stiffly beaten egg whites to the butter mixture. Pour into a well-greased funnel cake pan or bread pan, and bake in a 300 degree oven for 1 and 1/2 hours.

# Bourbon Walnut Pound Cake

| | |
|---|---|
| 2 cups finely chopped walnuts | 1/2 cup bourbon |
| 3 1/2 cups sifted all-purpose flour | 1 1/2 teaspoons baking powder |
| 1/2 teaspoon salt | 1/2 teaspoon nutmeg |
| 1/2 teaspoon cinnamon | 1/4 teaspoon cloves |
| 2 cups soft butter or margarine | 2 1/2 cups sugar |
| 8 eggs, well beaten | 1 teaspoon vanilla extract |
| 1/2 cup bourbon | |

Preheat oven to 350 degrees. Grease well, and flour a 10-inch tube pan. In small bowl, combine walnuts and 1/2 cup bourbon. Mix well. Let stand. Sift together flour, baking powder, salt, and spices. Set aside. In a large bowl, use an electric mixer on medium speed to beat butter with sugar until light. Add eggs and vanilla. Beat at high speed about 4 minutes, occasionally scraping side of bowl and guiding mixture into beaters with a rubber scraper until the mixture is thick and fluffy. At low speed, gradually beat in flour mixture just until combined. Stir in bourbon-walnut mixture. Turn batter into prepared pan, spreading evenly. Bake 1 hour and 10 minutes or until cake tester inserted in center comes out clean. Cool in pan on wire rack 15 minutes. Turn out of pan, and cool completely on wire rack. Soak cheesecloth in 1/2 cup bourbon. Wrap cake completely in cheesecloth; then in foil. Refrigerate several days. To serve, slice thinly. Makes 1 large pound cake.

 # Granny's Pound Cake

One pound of flour, one pound of sugar, one pound of butter, 8 eggs, 1 teaspoonful of rosewater and half a nutmeg.

# Brown Sugar Pound Cake

| | |
|---|---|
| 1 cup butter | 1/2 cup shortening |
| 1 pound light brown sugar | 1 cup granulated sugar |
| 5 eggs | 3 cups sifted flour |
| 1/2 teaspoon salt | 1 teaspoon baking powder |
| 1 cup milk | 1 teaspoon vanilla |
| 1 cup chopped walnuts | |

Beat butter and shortening together; add both sugars. Cream until light and fluffy. Beat in eggs, one at a time. Sift dry ingredients; add milk and vanilla alternately. Combine mixtures, and stir in nuts. Bake in tube pan for 1 hour and 45 minutes at 350 degrees. Prepare glaze and pour on hot cake.

**Walnut glaze:**

| | |
|---|---|
| 1 cup confectioners' sugar, sifted | 2 Tablespoons butter |
| 1/2 teaspoon of vanilla | 6 Tablespoons cream, or canned milk |
| 1/2 cup walnuts, chopped | |

Cream sugar and butter. Add cream, vanilla, and walnuts. Pour on hot cake.

 ## Minnehaha Cake

Two eggs, two teaspoonfuls of baking powder, one cup of sugar, one-half cup of butter, one-half cup of milk, one and one-half cups of flour. Beat the sugar with the butter. Bake in jelly-cake tins. *Filling:* Boil one cup of granulated sugar in water enough to moisten it, until it becomes ropy. Then place it in a basin of cold water to cool. Beat the white of one egg to a stiff froth, pour into the syrup and beat until cool; then add one cup of stoned raisins.

# Presbyterian Pound Cake

| | |
|---|---|
| 2 3/4 cups sugar | 1/2 pound butter |
| 1/2 cup shortening | 5 eggs |
| 1 cup milk | 3 cups plain flour |
| 1 teaspoon baking powder | 2 teaspoons almond, lemon, or vanilla extract |

Cream sugar, butter, and shortening together. On low speed of mixer, add in the following order the eggs, milk, flour, baking powder, and extract. Grease a bundt or tube pan. Pour in cake batter, and place in a cold oven. Set heat for 325 degrees. Bake approximately 1 1/2 hours.

*Mary S. Moss, Washington, North Carolina*

# Do Nothing Cake

| | |
|---|---|
| 2 cups flour | 2 cups sugar |
| 2 eggs, or 3, if small | 1 teaspoon vanilla |
| 1 teaspoon soda | 1/2 teaspoon salt |
| 1 small can crushed pineapple, include juice | coconut (optional) |

Mix all ingredients by hand. Pour in greased and floured 9x10-inch pan. Bake at 350 degrees for 30 to 40 minutes.

**Icing:**

| | |
|---|---|
| 1 stick margarine | 1 small can evaporated milk |
| 1 cup white sugar | coconut and nuts (optional) |

Combine margarine, milk, and sugar. Cook for 5 minutes. Remove from heat, and add coconut and crushed nuts if desired.

*Ann Proffitt Wine, Lynchburg, Virginia*

# Kentucky Whiskey Cake

| | | | |
|---|---|---|---|
| 5 | scant cups flour | 1 | pound white sugar |
| 1 | cup brown sugar | 3/4 | pound butter |
| 6 | eggs, separated and beaten | 1 | pint bourbon |
| 1 | teaspoon baking powder | 1 | pound pecan nut meats |
| 2 | teaspoons nutmeg | 1/2 | pound golden raisins, halved |
| 1 | pound red candied cherries, | | or 1/2 pound chopped dates, |
| | cut in half | | or 1/4 pound each |

Sift flour before measuring. Dredge pecans in a little of the flour, and set aside. Soak cherries, raisins, and/or dates overnight in bourbon. Cream butter and sugar until fluffy. Add egg yolks, and beat well. Mix in soaked fruit and remaining liquid. Add rest of flour, nutmeg, and baking powder to egg yolk mixture. Fold in beaten egg whites; add floured pecans. Heat oven to 250 degrees. Pour batter into large, greased tube pan that has been lined with greased paper. Bake 3 to 4 hours. When thoroughly cool, place in a container with tight fitting lid. Stuff center hole of cake with cheesecloth soaked in bourbon; wrap in heavy waxed paper. Cover, and when you serve it for the holidays, the cake will be moist and flavorful. It isn't necessary to add more whiskey while the cake is stored, but you may if you wish.

 ## Queen Cake

Two cupfuls of butter, two and a half cups of sugar, one and one-half pints of flour, 8 eggs, 1 teaspoonful of baking powder, one wine glass each of wine, brandy, and cream, teaspoonful each of extract of nutmeg, rose and lemon. One cup of currants, mashed, cup of raisins, stoned and cut in two, one cup of citron cut in small slices. Bake carefully in well-prepared tins in a moderate, steady oven one and one-half hours.

# Oatmeal Cake Squares

| | |
|---|---|
| 1   cup oatmeal, quick cooking | 1 1/2   cups boiling water |
| 1   stick margarine | 1   cup white sugar |
| 1   cup light brown sugar | 2   eggs |
| 1 1/2   cups self-rising flour | 1   teaspoon mace |
| 1   teaspoon soda | 1/4   teaspoon salt |

Sift mace, soda, salt, and flour. Pour boiling water over oatmeal which has been put in a large mixing bowl. Add margarine. Stir. Let stand until cool. Add sugar, eggs (not necessary to beat eggs), and dry ingredients. Mix thoroughly. (Electric beater will be fine.) Pour into greased 9x13-inch pan. Bake at 350 degrees for 35 to 45 minutes. Serves about 12.

**Topping:**

| | |
|---|---|
| 1   cup light brown sugar | 1   stick margarine |
| 1   egg | 2   Tablespoons milk |
| 1   cup coconut (canned, flaked) | 1   cup chopped nuts |

Place first 4 ingredients in saucepan. Stir, and cook slowly for about 5 minutes. Add coconut and nuts. Pour over cake while cake is hot. Then put in 500 degree oven or under broiler a few minutes. Watch it constantly.

*Mary S. Moss, Washington, North Carolina*

 # Pink Marble Cake

One cup of flour, one-half cup of cornstarch, one-half cup of butter, whites of four eggs, one cup of red sugar sand, one-half cup of milk, three-quarters of a teaspoonful of baking powder. Flavor to taste.

# Grandmother's Cake

| | | | |
|---|---|---|---|
| 1 | pound confectioners' sugar | 3 | sticks Parkay |
| 6 | eggs | 3 | cups plus 2 Tablespoons flour |
| | flavoring | | |

Cream Parkay and sugar with hand. Then beat in 1 egg at a time until all 6 are used. Divide flour into 4 parts and put in 1/4 at a time. Then add flavoring. If a little dry, add 2 or 3 tablespoons milk. Cook in tube pan 1 hour 15 minutes at 325 degrees.

*Annie Harrell Stewart, Charlotte, North Carolina*

# Carrot Cake

| | | | |
|---|---|---|---|
| 4 | eggs | 3 | cups grated carrots |
| 1 1/4 | cups oil | 2 | Tablespoons cinnamon |
| 2 | cups sugar | 1/2 | teaspoon soda |
| 1 | Tablespoon vanilla | 2 | cups self-rising flour |

Mix all ingredients. Pour into 3 round cake pans. Bake in a 350 degree oven for 20 minutes.

**Icing:**

| | | | |
|---|---|---|---|
| 1 | pound box powdered sugar | 1 | 8-ounce package cream |
| 1 | stick margarine, softened | | cheese, softened |
| 1 | Tablespoon vanilla | 1 | cup chopped pecans |

Mix together until smooth. Spread between layers and on top and sides of cake.

*Joann DeFilippo, Virginia Beach, Virginia*

# Pineapple Coconut Cake (Jim's Birthday Cake)

This cake was a result of combining my husband's two favorite cakes into one birthday cake. He enjoyed the cake so much that he wanted me to include the recipe in this book. M.D.

| | |
|---|---|
| 1 package white or yellow cake mix | 1 8-ounce can crushed pineapple, drained |
| 1 cup grated coconut | |

Prepare and bake cake as directed on cake mix box. Use 2 round, 8-inch layer pans. When cake has cooled, spread the pineapple and coconut on top of one layer. Cover with the first batch of icing. Place the other cake layer on top. Prepare the icing recipe again, and cover the top and sides of the cake.

**Icing:**

| | |
|---|---|
| 2 unbeaten egg whites | 1 1/2 cups sugar |
| 1/4 teaspoon cream of tartar | 5 tablespoons cold water |
| | 1 teaspoon vanilla or almond extract |

Mix first four ingredients in top of double boiler. Beat with electric mixer over boiling water for 7 minutes. Remove from heat, and add either vanilla or almond extract. After covering the bottom layer, make this recipe again, to cover the top layer and sides. I use vanilla in one icing recipe and almond extract in the other. The amount of pineapple and coconut can be increased or decreased according to preference.

*Mary Stewart Darden, Virginia Beach, Virginia*

# Icings

## Plain Frosting

| | |
|---|---|
| 1/8 teaspoon cream of tartar | 2 1/2 cups granulated sugar |
| 5 egg whites | 3/4 cup water |
| pinch of salt | 1 teaspoon lemon juice, or |
| | 1/8 teaspoon tartaric acid. |

Put 2 cups sugar in saucepan with water, and stir well. Cover with a plate. Never move the syrup while cooking. After reaching boiling point, then boil rapidly. Into the beaten whites of the eggs, add gradually 1/2 cup sugar. When syrup makes big bubbles, test it, and when it spins its first thread, it is done. Take off of fire and let cool. When it has stopped bubbling, pour slowly over the beaten whites. Put in double boiler and steam. Don't allow the water in lower boiler to touch the boiler that contains the icing. Add lemon juice or tartaric acid. If icing gets too thick, add a few drops of hot water.

## Ivory Frosting

| | |
|---|---|
| 2 egg whites, unbeaten | 1/4 cup brown sugar, packed |
| 1 1/4 cups granulated sugar | 5 Tablespoons water |
| 1 teaspoon vanilla | |

Combine egg whites, sugars, and water in top of double boiler, beating with rotary egg beater until thoroughly mixed. Place over rapidly boiling water; beat constantly with rotary beater, and cook 7 minutes or until frosting will stand in peaks. Remove from boiling water, add vanilla, and beat until thick enough to spread.

*Annie Harrell Stewart, Charlotte, North Carolina*

# Marshmallow Icing

2 cups sugar
1 Tablespoon vinegar
1/4 pound marshmallows

1 cup water
2 egg whites, well-beaten

Boil sugar, water, and vinegar until it threads. Stir in 2 well-beaten egg whites. Add marshmallows.

# Ranch Cake Icing

This is a good, quick, and easy recipe for a sheet cake. Mother would bake the cake ahead of time — usually while she was preparing dinner. It took just a few minutes to spread the icing on the cake, run it under the broiler, and serve the dessert. Perfect with ice cream or a cup of coffee! M.D.

2 cups brown sugar
  nuts

Carnation milk

Add just enough milk to brown sugar so it will spread. Add nuts. Spread on a partially cooled cake, and return to oven until icing bubbles.

*Mary S. Moss, Washington, North Carolina*

# Chocolate Icing

6 Tablespoons milk
1 Tablespoon cocoa
1 cup pecans, chopped

1 stick butter
1 box powdered sugar

Combine milk, butter, and cocoa. Bring to a boil. Remove from heat; add sugar. Mix well, and add pecan pieces. Pour over sheet cake while hot.

# Grandmother Proffitt's Caramel Filling

Annie Fox Proffitt, my husband's grandmother, used this recipe many years ago. Notes from her cookbook, published in 1890, are responsible for some of the delightful "granny" selections included in these pages. Annie was born in 1865. Sarah Lewis Fox, Annie's mother, had driven from Virginia into West Virginia to get her husband, Patrick Fox, who was being held in a Union Prisoner of War Camp. Apparently, the rough travel hastened Annie's birth, as she made her appearance in the back of the horse drawn cart being used for the journey. Annie's mother must certainly have suffered no lasting effects of the event, because 7 additional children were later born to Sarah and Patrick. M.P.

| | |
|---|---|
| 3 cups brown sugar | 3/4 cup butter |
| 3/4 cup cream | |

Boil ingredients together until thick enough to crack in water. Flavor with vanilla. Spread while hot between layers and over top and sides of cake.

*Annie Fox Proffitt, Lynchburg, Virginia*

# Fruit Nut Filling

| | |
|---|---|
| 1/3 cup chopped dates | 1/3 cup chopped raisins |
| 3/4 cup sugar | 1 cup water |
| 1/3 cup walnuts | 1 Tablespoon lemon juice |
| 1 teaspoon grated lemon rind | |

Combine dates, raisins, sugar, and water in saucepan. Cook over low flame 15 minutes or until thick enough to spread, stirring constantly. Cool. Add nuts, lemon juice, and rind. Chill before spreading on cake.

*Annie Harrell Stewart, Charlotte, North Carolina*

# Grandmother Stewart's Caramel Filling

Every Christmas dinner and sometimes for other special occasions, we would have a caramel cake. We were always told it was Grandmother's wonderful recipe, and it wouldn't be Christmas without a cake with this special icing. It was truly a family favorite! M.D.

| | |
|---|---|
| 1  1-pound box light brown sugar | 1/3  pound butter |
| milk (1/3 cup approx.) | 1  teaspoon vanilla |

Mix the brown sugar and milk in a pot . Let this boil up good before adding butter. Cook until soft ball forms when dropped in cold water. Beat thoroughly. Add the vanilla. It hardens very quickly, so keep it warm until finished.

*Annie Harrell Stewart, Charlotte, North Carolina*

# Seven Minute Icing

| | |
|---|---|
| 1 3/4  cups of sugar | 5  Tablespoons water |
| 2  egg whites, unbeaten | 1  teaspoon cream of tartar |

Put all together in a double boiler. Put over boiling water, and beat with rotary beater exactly 7 minutes. Remove from heat; beat until it will stand in peaks.

# Coconut Icing

| | |
|---|---|
| 1 1/2  cups sugar | 1/3  cup orange juice |
| 2  egg whites, unbeaten | coconut |

Use same directions as for Seven Minute Icing. (See above recipe.)

# Lemon Filling

2   cups sugar
3   lemons, rind and juice

1 to 2   cups water
2   egg whites

Boil water and sugar together to soft ball stage. Beat egg whites until very stiff. Slowly pour hot liquid into beaten egg whites; add rind and lemon juice last. Spread between layers and over top and sides of cakes.

# Cream Cheese Frosting

1   8-ounce package cream
    cheese
1   teaspoon vanilla
    chopped nuts

1/2   stick margarine
1   box powdered sugar
    few drops of milk

In a chilled bowl, beat cream cheese with margarine. Gradually add powdered sugar. Stir in vanilla; mix well. Add a little milk, if needed. Spread on cake and sprinkle nuts over top.

# Mocha Frosting

1/3   cup butter or margarine
2   squares unsweetened,
    chocolate, melted

3   cups confectioners' sugar
1/4   cup (about) strong, cold
    coffee

Cream butter or margarine until very soft. Continue to cream while adding in half of the sugar. Add chocolate; mix well. Gradually stir in rest of sugar. Add coffee 1 tablespoon at a time until frosting is fluffy and easy to spread. Makes enough to fill and frost a 2-layer cake.

# Candies and Cookies

## Candies

## Fondant Candy

Into one tumbler, put the white of an egg, and, in a second tumbler, water reaching to the same height. Combine in a mixing bowl, and add confectioners' sugar enough to make a consistency that will mold, stirring well. Use this mixture, called fondant, in making various candies as follows: Make balls the size of marbles, and put between halves of English walnuts, pecans, or butternuts, which press together so that a rounded edge of the fondant extends beyond the nut meats. Make tiny balls of the fondant, and with them stuff candied cherries. Make larger balls to stuff dates or small figs. Mix chopped nuts with a part of the fondant, place on a molding board dusted with the sugar, roll until half an inch thick, cut into squares, dip in granulated sugar, making "nut hamlins." Make some of the fondant into thimble-sized balls, and dip, using a wooden toothpick, into unsweetened melted chocolate; place on paraffin paper to cool. There is hardly any limit to the goodies you can concoct in the candy line with this foundation. Birch-bark boxes, lined with fancy paper, make pretty containers.

*Annie Harrell Stewart, Charlotte, North Carolina*

## Marshmallow Drops

Dissolve one-half pound of gum arabic in one pint of water; strain and add one-half pound of white sugar, and place over the fire, stirring constantly until the syrup is dissolved and of the consistency of honey; then add gradually the whites of four eggs well beaten. Stir the mixture until it becomes somewhat thin and does not adhere to the fingers. Flavor to taste, and pour all into a pan slightly dusted with powdered starch, and when cool, divide into small squares.

## Sea Foam Candy

3 cups white sugar
1 cup water
1 Tablespoon fresh lemon juice
   nuts, chopped

1/2 cup Blue Label Karo Syrup
3 egg whites, stiffly beaten
1 teaspoon vanilla

Cook sugar, syrup, and water until it spins a thread. Pour over stiffly beaten egg whites. Add lemon juice, vanilla, and nuts. Drop by spoonfuls on waxed paper.

*Mary S. Moss, Washington, North Carolina*

## Divinity Fudge

2 2/3 cups white sugar
  2/3 cup water
    1 cup chopped almonds

2 2/3 cups Karo Blue Label syrup
    2 egg whites, beaten

Combine sugar, syrup, and water. Boil until it will make a bead in cold water. Pour over the beaten egg whites, add the almonds, and beat. Pour into a buttered dish, and cut into squares when cool.

*Annie Harrell Stewart, Charlotte, North Carolina*

## Fudgemallow Candy

1 12-ounce package semi-sweet
   chocolate pieces

4 cups miniature marshmallows
1 cup chunky peanut butter

Melt chocolate pieces with peanut butter in saucepan over low heat, stirring until smooth. Fold in marshmallows. Pour into greased 9-inch square pan; chill until firm. Cut into squares.

# Fabulous Fudge

| | |
|---|---|
| 2 1/4 cups sugar | 3/4 cup evaporated milk |
| 16 large marshmallows, or | 1/4 cup butter or margarine |
| 1 cup marshmallow creme | 1/4 teaspoon salt |
| 1 6-ounce package Hershey's | 1 cup chopped pecans |
| semi-sweet chocolate pieces | 1 teaspoon vanilla |

Mix sugar, milk, marshmallows, butter, and salt in heavy 2-quart saucepan.
Cook over medium heat to a boil, stirring constantly. Boil, and stir 5 minutes
more. Take off heat. Add chocolate pieces, and stir until melted. Stir in
pecans and vanilla. Spread in 8-inch buttered pan, and cut into squares when
cool.

*Sara S. Gabel, Washington, North Carolina*

# Fudge Candy

| | |
|---|---|
| 3 cups white sugar | 3 squares chocolate |
| 1/2 cup white syrup | 1 cup Carnation milk or 1 small |
| 1 Tablespoon butter | can plus a little water |
| 1 teaspoon vanilla | |

Mix sugar, chocolate, syrup, and milk together. Cook over slow heat. Don't
let it boil until after sugar and chocolate have dissolved. Stir often; cook until
a small amount dropped into water forms a soft ball. Mix in butter and vanilla,
but don't beat until mixture has cooled. Then beat until it creams (a long time).

*Mary S. Moss, Washington, North Carolina*

# Aunt Seignie Jennette's Chocolate Fudge

Mother always said this was the best fudge she had ever eaten, and that Aunt Seignie was just as sweet as the fudge she made.   M.D.

| | |
|---|---|
| 1   pound light brown sugar | 3   squares chocolate |
| 1/2   of a tall can of milk | 1/2   jar of marshmallow creme |
| nuts, if desired | |

Melt chocolate.  Add sugar and milk.  Cook to soft ball stage.  Remove from stove.  Add marshmallow creme.  Add nuts, if desired.  Beat until it is ready to pour.  It takes lots of beating.

# Million Dollar Fudge

| | |
|---|---|
| 4  1/2   cups sugar | pinch salt |
| 2   Tablespoons butter | 1   tall can evaporated milk |
| 1   12-ounce package semi-sweet chocolate bits | 1   12-ounce package German sweet chocolate |
| 1   pint marshmallow creme | 2   cups nut meats |

In a saucepan, combine sugar, salt, butter, and milk and boil for 6 minutes.  In a large bowl, combine the chocolates, marshmallow creme, and nuts.  Pour boiling syrup over these ingredients, and beat until the chocolate is melted. Pour into a pan to cool.  Let stand a few hours before cutting.  Place in a tin box, and store in a cool place.

*Elsie Lockhart, Roanoke, Virginia*

# Peanut Butter Fudge

2  cups sugar
1  cup crunchy peanut butter
1  teaspoon vanilla

1 1/2  cups marshmallow creme
2/3  cup milk

Cook sugar with milk to soft ball stage.  Add remaining ingredients; stir until well-blended.  Turn mixture into 9x9-inch buttered pan.  Cut into squares. Makes 2 pounds.

*Kempsville High School, Virginia Beach, Virginia*

# Microwave Pecan Brittle

1  cup granulated sugar
1  cup pecan pieces
1  teaspoon vanilla

1/2  cup white corn syrup
1  teaspoon butter
1  teaspoon baking soda

In 1 1/2-quart casserole, stir together sugar and syrup.  Cook in microwave on high setting for 4 minutes.  Stir in pecan pieces.  Microwave on high 3 to 5 minutes, until light brown.  Add butter and vanilla to syrup, blending well. Microwave on high 1 to 2 minutes more.  Pecans will be lightly browned and syrup very hot.  Add soda, and gently stir until light and foamy.  Pour mixture onto lightly greased cookie sheet or unbuttered nonstick cookie sheet.  Let cool 1/2 to 1 hour.  When cool, break in small pieces, and store in airtight container. (Cooking times may vary with the wattage of your microwave.)

*Janie Proffitt Flippo, Roanoke, Virginia*

 # Corn Balls

Boil one cupful of molasses and two tablespoonfuls of sugar twenty minutes. When done, rub one-half of a teaspoonful of soda smooth; then stir in popcorn. Butter the hands, and ball.

# Pralines

2 cups light brown sugar
2 cups small pecan pieces

1/4 cup butter
1/4 cup water

Combine sugar and butter with water. Set candy thermometer in pan. Cook over low heat until mixture boils, stirring continuously. Add pecans, and cook until temperature reaches 248 degrees, stirring all the while. Remove from heat; drop by tablespoonfuls into a buttered shallow pan. Makes about 1 pound.

# Peanut Butter Chewy

1/2 cup sugar
1/2 cup peanut butter
2 Tablespoons milk
1 teaspoon soda
1 3/4 cups rolled oats
1/2 teaspoon salt

1/2 cup margarine
1 egg
1/2 cup brown sugar
1 3/4 cups flour
1 teaspoon vanilla

Cream together sugars, margarine, peanut butter, egg, and milk. Add rest of ingredients. Mix well. If batter seems too stiff, add a little more milk. Bake at 350 degrees in a 9 x 12-inch pan until done.

*Central Office, Virginia Beach, Virginia School System*

 # Candy for Children

Take equal parts of nuts, raisins, dates, and figs, if desired. Grind them in the meat chopper. Mix all together and form into balls about the size of walnuts. Roll balls in powdered or granulated sugar and wrap each ball in a small piece of oiled paper, twisting both ends of paper. Eat them after lunch or dinner — not between meals.

*Annie Harrell Stewart, Charlotte, North Carolina*

# Sugar Coated Peanuts

1 cup granulated sugar      1/2 cup water
2 cups raw, shelled peanuts,
   skin on

Dissolve sugar in water in saucepan over medium heat. Add peanuts; continue to cook over medium heat, stirring frequently. Cook until peanuts are completely sugared. Nuts should be coated, with no syrup remaining in pan. Pour mixture onto ungreased cookie sheet, separating peanuts, and bake in a 300 degree oven for approximately 30 minutes. Stir at 5 minute intervals.

# Noodle Candy

This recipe came to me from a student teacher with whom I worked early in my teaching career. My children were small then, and it was wonderful to have a recipe that they liked and that could be prepared so quickly. M.P.

1 large can Chinese noodles      1 cup nuts, your choice
18 ounces butterscotch morsels

Melt morsels in double boiler; then mix other ingredients. Drop by spoonfuls onto waxed paper.

# Peanut Candy

3 cups sugar      3/4 cup Karo Syrup
   butter, size of walnut      1 cup water
3 cups peanuts, crushed      1/3 cup evaporated milk

Dissolve sugar in water. Add syrup and cook until it spins a thread. Beat in milk and butter; stir in peanuts. Pour onto buttered dish. Before completely cooled, cut into squares.

# Cookies

## Nutty Fingers

Mother made these every Christmas. My children love them as much as I do, and my sister and I continue the tradition of making nutty fingers every December. M.D.

| | |
|---|---|
| 1 1/4 sticks butter, or oleo | 4 Tablespoons confectioners' sugar |
| 1 Tablespoon cold water | |
| 1 teaspoon vanilla | 2 cups flour, sifted |
| 1 cup nuts, chopped | confectioners' sugar |

Cream together butter, sugar, water, and vanilla. Add flour and nuts. Shape into fingers. Place on a lightly greased baking sheet. Bake in 325 degree oven for about 15 minutes. Let cool in pan. When cool, roll in confectioners' sugar.

*Mary S. Moss, Washington, North Carolina*

## Chocolate Chip Cookies

| | |
|---|---|
| 1 package Duncan Hines White Deluxe Cake mix | 1/2 cup vegetable oil |
| | 2 Tablespoons water |
| 2 eggs | 1 6-ounce package semi-sweet chocolate bits |
| 1/2 cup nuts, chopped | |

Preheat oven to 350 degrees. Blend cake mix, oil, water, and eggs. Stir in chocolate bits and nuts. Drop from teaspoon onto ungreased cookie sheet. Bake for 10 to 12 minutes. Cool on cookie sheet for 1 minute.

# Toffee Bars

1/2 pound butter
2 cups plain flour
1 cup nuts, chopped
1 teaspoon vanilla

1 cup light brown sugar
1 6-ounce package chocolate
  bits

Cream together butter and sugar. Mix in flour, chocolate bits, nuts, and vanilla. Spoon into ungreased 9 x 12-inch pan; pat smooth. Bake in 350 degree oven for 25 minutes. While hot, cut into bars.

*Mary S. Moss, Washington, North Carolina*

# Fudge Squares

1 stick butter
3 eggs
3/4 cup cocoa
1 cup nut meats

1 1/4 cups sugar
1 cup flour
1 teaspoon baking powder
1 teaspoon vanilla

Cream butter and sugar. Add eggs, unbeaten, one at a time. In another bowl, mix flour, cocoa, and baking powder. Add to butter and sugar mixture. Stir in nuts and vanilla. Spread onto greased pan, and cook in 350 degree oven 30 minutes. Cut into squares.

*Annie Harrell Stewart, Charlotte, North Carolina*

# Pie Crust Cookies

1 package pie crust mix
1 egg

1 cup brown sugar

Beat egg, and mix with sugar and pie crust mix.. Form into roll. Chill, and slice. Bake in 350 degree oven. Nuts may be added, if desired.

*Mary S. Moss, Washington, North Carolina*

# Bake and Forget 'em

| | |
|---|---|
| 2 egg whites | 2/3 cup sugar |
| 1/2 teaspoon vanilla | 1 6-ounce package chocolate |
| 1 cup nuts, chopped | bits |

Important!  Preheat oven to 350 degrees, line pan with foil, and grease before preparing recipe.  Beat egg whites until stiff.  Continue to beat, gradually adding sugar and vanilla.  Fold in chocolate bits and nuts.  Drop by spoonfuls onto cookie sheet lined with greased aluminum foil.  Place in preheated oven. Turn oven off and leave for 5 to 6 hours or overnight if possible, until thoroughly cooled.  Makes about 2 dozen.  Recipe can be easily doubled.

*Mary S. Moss, Washington, North Carolina*

# Brownies

These are delicious!  This recipe is from a friend who truly enjoys cooking. M.D.

| | |
|---|---|
| 4 squares chocolate | 1/2 cup butter |
| 4 eggs | 1/4 teaspoon salt |
| 2 cups sugar | 2 teaspoons vanilla |
| 1 cup flour, sifted | 1 cup nuts, chopped |

Melt together chocolate and butter.  Cool.  Beat eggs until light; add salt.  Add sugar gradually, and beat until light and creamy.  Fold into chocolate mixture. Add vanilla and 1 cup sifted flour.  Beat until smooth and light.  Fold in nuts. Pour in buttered and floured 9x13-inch pan.  Bake for 25 to 30 minutes in a 325 degree oven.

*Joan Manuel, Virginia Beach, Virginia*

# Sour Cream Brownies

| | |
|---|---|
| 1 cup margarine | 1 cup water |
| 4 Tablespoons cocoa | 2 cups flour |
| 2 cups sugar | 1/2 teaspoon salt |
| 2 eggs | 1/2 cup sour cream |
| 1 teaspoon baking soda | |

In a saucepan, bring margarine, water, and cocoa to a boil. Do not cool.
Combine flour, sugar, and salt in mixing bowl; add the hot cocoa mixture.
Beat in the eggs, sour cream, and soda. Pour in a greased pan, and bake at
350 degrees for 30 minutes. Frost while hot.

**Frosting:**

| | |
|---|---|
| 1 cup margarine | 4 Tablespoons cocoa |
| 6 Tablespoons milk | 3 1/2 cups powdered sugar |
| 1 teaspoon vanilla | 1 cup nuts, chopped |

In a saucepan, bring margarine, cocoa, and milk to a boil, stirring constantly.
While hot, add the sugar, nuts, and vanilla. Spread on hot brownies. Cool,
and cut into squares.

# Nut Cookies

| | |
|---|---|
| 1 cup nuts, grated | 1/2 cup margarine or butter |
| 2 Tablespoons granulated sugar | 1 teaspoon vanilla |
| 1 cup cake flour | powdered sugar |

Cream margarine, and add sugar. Add flour, nuts, and vanilla; mix well. Drop
by spoon onto lightly greased cookie sheet. Bake 10 to 15 minutes in 325
degree oven. Roll in powdered sugar while still hot and again when cooled.

# Chocolate Syrup Brownies

| | |
|---|---|
| 1/2  cup butter or margarine | 1  cup sugar |
| 2  eggs | 1  cup all purpose flour, sifted |
| 1/4  teaspoon baking soda | 3/4  cup chocolate syrup, canned |
| 1  teaspoon vanilla | 3/4  cup nuts, chopped |

Cream butter and sugar until light and fluffy. Add eggs one at a time, beating after each addition. Sift flour and soda together. Add alternately with the chocolate syrup to creamed mixture. Blend in vanilla and nuts. Pour into a greased and floured 9x13x2-inch pan. Bake at 350 degrees for 40 to 45 minutes.

**Frosting:**

| | |
|---|---|
| 1/4  cup butter or margarine, softened | 1/4  cup canned chocolate syrup |
| | 2  cups sifted powdered sugar |

Blend butter and chocolate. Gradually blend in sugar. Spread on top of cooled brownies. Cut into squares.

*Sara S. Gabel, Washington, North Carolina*

# Nellie Faye's Date Bars

| | |
|---|---|
| 1  box light brown sugar | 2  cups flour |
| 4  eggs | 1  cup nuts, chopped |
| 1/2  package dates, chopped | |

Mix in order: sugar, flour, eggs, nuts, dates. Pour into greased 9x13-inch pan. Bake in 350 degree oven for 20 minutes or until top lightly browns. Cool and cut into squares.

# No-Bake Delight Bars

|   |   |   |   |
|---|---|---|---|
| | whole graham crackers | 2 | sticks margarine |
| 1 | cup sugar | 1 | cup milk |
| 1 | egg, beaten | 1 | cup graham cracker crumbs |
| 1/2 | cup coconut | 1/2 | cup nuts, chopped |

Line bottom of 9x13-inch pan with whole graham crackers. Cook together margarine, sugar, milk, and beaten egg. Cook until mixture coats spoon. Let cool. Stir in graham cracker crumbs, coconut, and nuts. Pour over whole crackers already in pan; top with another layer of whole crackers. Coat with glaze.

**Glaze:**

|   |   |   |   |
|---|---|---|---|
| 1 | cup powdered sugar | 2 | Tablespoons margarine |
| 1 | teaspoon vanilla | | warm water |

Melt margarine, and stir in sugar and vanilla. Add just enough warm water so that it will spread easily. Cut, and remove from pan with spatula.

# Black Walnut Ice-Box Cookies

|   |   |   |   |
|---|---|---|---|
| 1/2 | pound melted butter | 1 | cup white sugar |
| 2 | eggs | 1 | cup brown sugar |
| 1 | Tablespoon cinnamon | 3 | cups flour |
| 1 | teaspoon soda | 2 | teaspoons vanilla |
| 1 | cup black walnuts, chopped | | |

Beat eggs, and combine with melted butter. Mix in other ingredients; form into a roll. Wrap roll in waxed paper, and refrigerate until very cold. Cut into thin slices. Bake on a cookie sheet for 10 minutes in a 375 degree oven.

# Lemon Bars

| | | | |
|---|---|---|---|
| 1 | cup flour | 1/2 | cup melted butter |
| 2 | eggs | 1 | cup pecans, chopped |
| 1 1/2 | cups brown sugar | 2 | Tablespoons flour |
| 1/2 | teaspoon baking powder | 1/3 | teaspoon salt |
| 1 | teaspoon vanilla | | glaze |

Combine 1 cup flour and melted butter; spread in bottom of a 9x12-inch pan. Bake for 12 minutes in a 350 degree oven. Combine other ingredients, and spread on top of baked crust. Bake for 25 minutes in a 350 degree oven.

**Glaze:**

| | | | |
|---|---|---|---|
| 1 | cup powdered sugar | 2 | Tablespoons lemon juice |

Mix well; spread while hot, before cutting into bars

# Macadamia Nut Balls

| | | | |
|---|---|---|---|
| 1 | cup butter or margarine | 1/2 | cup granulated sugar |
| 1 | teaspoon vanilla | 2 1/4 | cups all-purpose flour, |
| 1/4 | teaspoon salt | | sifted |
| 1 | cup macadamia nuts, | | confectioners' sugar |
| | finely chopped | | |

Preheat oven to 350 degrees. In a large bowl with electric mixer on medium speed, cream butter until fluffy. Gradually beat in sugar and vanilla. Sift flour with salt; stir into mixture. Stir in nuts until well distributed. Shape mixture into 1-inch balls, and place on ungreased cookie sheets. Bake 12 minutes or until cookies just start to brown. (Cookies should remain light in color.) Let cool a few minutes on cookie sheet. While still warm, roll in confectioners' sugar. Makes about 3 1/2 dozen.

*Sara S. Gabel, Washington, North Carolina*

# Desserts

## Angel Food Cake Dessert

Be sure to prepare this the day before, or at least several hours before you plan to serve it.  This is an especially pretty dessert served either on a plate or prepared and served in a clear bowl (like trifle).  M.D.

| | | | |
|---|---|---|---|
| 1 | large angel food cake | 6 | lemons |
| 6 | eggs, separated | 1 | cup sugar |
| 1 | envelope Knox gelatin | 3/4 | cup sugar, or less |
| 1/4 | cup cold water | | |

Break cake into pieces about 1 inch in size.  Extract juice from all of the lemons, and grate rind of 1 or 2 of them.  Beat egg yolks, add 1 cup sugar, and beat again.  Add lemon juice and grated rind.  Cook in double boiler until slightly thick.  Remove from stove.  Soften gelatin in 1/4 cup cold water; add to mixture.  Beat egg whites until stiff.  Beat in 3/4 cup or less of sugar.  Fold egg whites into cooked mixture.  Oil tube cake pan with vegetable oil.  Put a layer of cake pieces in bottom of pan; add a layer of lemon sauce mixture.  Continue alternating layers, finishing with lemon sauce.  Place in refrigerator overnight.  Run knife around edge of pan; turn cake out onto a large plate or platter.  Cover with slightly sweetened whipped cream.

*Mary S. Moss, Washington, North Carolina*

# Minted Angel Allegretti

| | |
|---|---|
| 1 angel food cake | 2 1/2 cups miniature marsh-mallows |
| 1/2 cup milk | |
| 1 cup creme de menthe | 1/4 teaspoon salt |
| 4 to 6 drops green food coloring | 1 pint chilled whipping cream |
| 1 1-ounce package melted chocolate (Baker's) | |

Split cake into 3 layers. Heat marshmallows and milk over medium heat, stirring occasionally until marshmallows are melted — about 5 minutes. Remove from heat; cool at room temperature until thickened — about 20 to 25 minutes. Stir in creme de menthe, salt, and food coloring. Beat whipping cream in chilled small bowl until stiff peaks form. Fold into marshmallow mixture. Stack cake layers, filling each with 1 cup of the filling. Frost sides of cake with filling that is left. Drizzle chocolate around the top edge of cake, allowing to run down the sides. Refrigerate until serving time.

*Helen Stewart, Shallotte, North Carolina*

 # Tipsy Cake No. 1

Make a velvet sponge cake the day before. Make a boiled custard as follows: To 1 quart of milk, add four tablespoonfuls of sugar, the yolks of 4 eggs and the whites of 2. Boil the milk and pour slowly over the eggs and sugar. Place on the stove and cook, stirring constantly, until it becomes a little thick. Remove from the fire. Strain and flavor with vanilla. Have ready 1 pint of cream, slightly sweetened, and 1/2 pound of blanched almonds. Break the sponge cake into pieces and put a layer of the pieces in a large bowl, stick thickly with the almonds. Saturate with good scuppernong wine or claret. Pour over some of the custard and then some of the whipped cream. Add another layer of cake and proceed in the same way until as many layers are used as you wish. Lastly, pour over the remaining custard and pile the whipped cream on top.

# Tipsy Cake No. 2

| | | | |
|---|---|---|---|
| 1 | angel food cake | 1/2 | pound butter |
| 1 | pound confectioners' sugar | 5 | egg yolks |
| 1/2 | cup bourbon whiskey | 1 | cup pecans, chopped |
| 1/4 | pound macaroon crumbs, if desired | | |

Split angel food cake into 3 layers. In a bowl, cream butter, and add sugar slowly. Beat well. Add egg yolks, one at a time, beating well between each. Add bourbon, pecans, and macaroon crumbs. Put this filling between the layers. Cover cake; refrigerate for a day or two. Frost just before serving.

**Frosting:**

| | | | |
|---|---|---|---|
| 1 | pint cream, whipped | 2 | Tablespoons sugar |
| 2 | Tablespoons whiskey | 1/4 | pound almonds, toasted and chopped |
| 1/4 | pound macaroon crumbs | | |

Combine whipped cream, sugar, and whiskey. Frost cake. Sprinkle almonds and macaroon crumbs on top.

# Biscuit Tortoni

| | | | |
|---|---|---|---|
| 2 1/2 | cups crushed macaroon cookies | 1 | large can mixed, salted nuts, chopped |
| 6 | Tablespoons candied cherries or maraschino cherries | 1/2 | gallon vanilla ice cream |

Place softened ice cream into large bowl. Pour other ingredients on top, and stir. Quickly spoon dessert into crinkled baking cups which have been placed in muffin tins. Put in freezer until serving time.

*Sara S. Gabel, Washington, North Carolina*

# Chocolate Eclair Dessert

| | |
|---|---|
| 1 large package instant vanilla pudding mix | 1 1/2 cups milk |
| 1 box graham crackers | 1 large container Cool Whip |

Mix pudding with milk. Fold in the Cool Whip. Put layer of crackers in bottom of 9x13-inch pan. Add layer of pudding. Continue layers, ending with graham crackers. Top with glaze.

**Glaze:**

| | |
|---|---|
| 1 cup sugar | 1/3 cup cocoa |
| 1/4 cup milk | 1 stick margarine |
| 1 teaspoon vanilla | |

In a saucepan, combine sugar, cocoa, and milk. Bring to a boil; boil for 1 minute. Remove from heat, and add margarine and vanilla. Cool completely. Spread over top layer of graham crackers. Refrigerate overnight.

*Mary S. Moss, Washington, North Carolina*

# Texas Pudding Dessert

| | |
|---|---|
| 4 egg yolks | 1/2 cup sugar |
| 1/2 cup sherry wine | 1 pint cream |
| 4 egg whites | 1 cup pecans, chopped |
| 1 slice crystallized pineapple | 1 bottle red cherries, without juice |

Cook egg yolks, sugar, and sherry wine in double boiler until thick. Cool. Whip cream and egg whites separately; then combine, and mix with cooked mixture. Add pecans, pineapple, and cherries. Freeze. Serve with plain cookies or cake. For 8 to 10.

*Annie Harrell Stewart, Charlotte, North Carolina*

# Three Layered Dessert

I first prepared this with chocolate pudding mix and shared it with my friend and neighbor Helen Clark. Helen made the dessert using lemon pudding, and that was delicious too. This dessert would be good using any flavor of pudding! M.D.

| | |
|---|---|
| 1 stick butter | 1 cup flour |
| 1 cup pecans, chopped | 1 8-ounce package cream |
| 1 cup powdered sugar | cheese |
| 1 cup Cool Whip | 2 packages instant chocolate |
| 3 cups milk | pudding |

Cream butter, flour, and pecans. Pat into bottom of 9x12-inch pan or glass baking dish. Bake at 350 degrees for 25 minutes. Cool. Mix cream cheese, sugar, and Cool Whip. Spread over first layer. Mix chocolate pudding with milk until thick. Pour over first two layers. Put remaining Cool Whip on top. Sprinkle with nuts. Chill for several hours before serving.

*Mary Stewart Darden, Virginia Beach, Virginia*

 ## Grandmother's Strawberries

Use equal weights of sugar and strawberries. Put the strawberries in the preserving kettle in layers, sprinkling sugar over each layer. The fruit and sugar should not be more than 4 inches deep. Place the kettle on the stove, and heat the fruit and sugar slowly to the boiling point. When it begins to boil, skim carefully. Boil ten minutes, counting from the time the fruit begins to bubble. Pour the cooked fruit into platters, having it about 2 or 3 inches deep. Place the platters in a sunny window, in an unused room, for three or four days. In that time the fruit will grow plump and firm, and the syrup will thicken almost to a jelly. Put this preserve, cold, into jars or tumblers.

*Annie Harrell Stewart, Charlotte, North Carolina*

# Java-Rum Torte

| | |
|---|---|
| 1/2 cup sugar | 1/2 cup water |
| 2 Tablespoons instant coffee | 2 Tablespoons rum |
| 1 Tablespoon butter or margarine | 1 prepared loaf pound cake |
| | 1 envelope dessert topping mix |

Prepare dessert topping according to directions. In small saucepan, combine sugar, water, and coffee crystals. Bring to boil, and boil hard for 3 minutes, stirring occasionally. Remove from heat; stir in rum and butter. Cool for 5 minutes. Slice cake lengthwise into 3 layers. Slowly spoon 3 tablespoons of the coffee mixture over bottom layer. Spread on 1/3 of the prepared topping. Repeat with middle layer, and stack atop bottom layer. Spoon 3 tablespoons coffee mixture atop cut surface of top layer. Invert and place atop other two layers. Spread remaining whipped topping over top. Bring remaining coffee mixture to boil for 1 minute, stirring constantly. Cool 5 to 10 minutes, and drizzle over top of torte. Chill. Makes 8 to 10 servings.

 # Old South Ambrosia

| | |
|---|---|
| 1 fresh coconut. | 5 oranges |
| 1 can crushed pineapple, with juice | 1 can fruit cocktail, with juice |
| 2 apples, chopped | 2 bananas, sliced |
| 1/2 cup pecans, coarsely broken | sugar, to taste |
| cherries | |

Grate coconut in a bowl. Add peeled and sectioned oranges; discard membrane and seeds. Add pineapple, fruit cocktail, apples, bananas, and nuts. Sweeten with sugar, being careful not to add too much as the syrup from the fruit is usually sufficient. Chill before serving. This dessert is pretty garnished with cherries and served in a crystal bowl.

# Orange Chiffon Dessert

| | |
|---|---|
| 1 orange chiffon cake | 1 pint cream |
| 1 package vanilla instant pudding | 1 large can crushed pineapple |

Split cake across in 3 layers. Cream should be whipped but should not be too thick. Fold, do not whip, prepared pudding into whipped cream. Add pineapple with juice to mixture. Spread between layers of cake and over entire cake. Chill several hours.

*Mary S. Moss, Washington, North Carolina*

# Pineapple Delight

Cream together 1 tablespoon butter, 2/3 cup sugar, and 1 egg. Add 1 large can crushed pineapple, 1 small box vanilla wafers, and 1/2 cup nuts. Mix well and chill.

 # "New Dessert"

| | |
|---|---|
| 4 Tablespoons orange juice | 4 Tablespoons lemon juice |
| 2/3 cup sugar | 3 egg yolks, beaten |
| 3 egg whites, beaten | 1 small can evaporated milk |
| vanilla wafers | |

Mix juices, sugar, and well-beaten egg yolks, and cook in double boiler until thick. Fold mixture into egg whites which have been beaten until stiff. Whip a small can of milk until stiff and add to mixture. Have milk and bowl in which you whip it very cold — it won't whip otherwise. Line refrigerator pan with crushed vanilla wafers. Pour mixture on this. Cover with crushed vanilla wafers. Chill or freeze. I prefer it about half frozen. Serves 6 or 8 and costs about 20 or 25 cents.

*Annie Harrell Stewart, Charlotte, North Carolina*

# Charlotte Russe

A number of years ago, I was served Mrs. McCowen's Charlotte Russe following dinner at my sister's home in Richmond. I thought at the time it was one of
the best desserts I had ever eaten, and I still think that! My sister's mother-in-
law, Nancy McCowen, graciously permitted me to include the recipe in this
book. M.D.

| | | | |
|---|---|---|---|
| 1 | dozen lady fingers | 1 | envelope gelatin |
| 2 | Tablespoons cold water | 1/2 | cup milk |
| 3 | eggs, whites and yolks beaten | 1 | cup XXXX sugar |
| | separately | 1 | teaspoon vanilla |
| 1 | pint heavy cream, divided | 2 | Tablespoons XXXX sugar |

Dissolve gelatin in 2 tablespoons cold water. Heat the milk. Do not boil. Add
gelatin, and cool. Beat egg yolks well; add the sugar and vanilla. Cream well.
Fold in well-beaten egg whites, and then gelatin mixture. Fold in 1/2 pint
cream that has been whipped. Important: Let stand 3 minutes. Fold well
again. Repeat this two more times. Split the lady fingers, and line sides of a
2-quart bowl with them, flat side next to the bowl, each one touching the other.
Pour in the custard mixture, and put in refrigerator. An hour before serving,
whip 1/2 pint heavy cream, adding 2 Tablespoons XXXX sugar gradually.
Spread over custard mixture. Keep chilled in refrigerator.

*Nancy McCowen, Naples Florida*

# Pineapple Sherbet

| | | | |
|---|---|---|---|
| 1 | can Carnation milk, whipped | 3/4 | cup sugar |
| | pinch salt | 2 | Tablespoons lemon juice |
| 1 | small can crushed pineapple | | |

Mix all ingredients and freeze. Crushed peaches may be used instead of pineapple, but use less lemon juice.

*Annie Harrell Stewart, Charlotte, North Carolina*

# Trifle

| | | | |
|---|---|---|---|
| 18 | lady fingers | 6 | almond macaroons, |
| | raspberry jam | | cut in small pieces |
| 1 | cup boiled custard | 1/2 | cup sherry |
| 2 | Tablespoons milk | 2 | Tablespoons slivered |
| 2 | egg whites, whipped | | almonds, blanched |
| 2 or 3 | Tablespoons sugar | | |

Open lady fingers; spread jam on half. Close. Place on bottom of a deep glass or silver dish. Cover with macaroon pieces. Mix the sherry and milk; pour over lady fingers and macaroons. Stick in slivered almonds. Let stand for an hour. Pour custard over all, and top with meringue made from egg whites which have been beaten with sugar.

# Date Delight

| | | | |
|---|---|---|---|
| 1 | cup whipping cream | 3 | Tablespoons confectioners' |
| 1 | teaspoon vanilla | | sugar |
| 1/2 | cup dates, chopped | 1/2 | cup walnuts, broken |
| 12 | graham crackers, crushed | | dash of salt |
| 4 | maraschino cherries | | |

Whip cream until stiff; fold in sugar, vanilla, dates, nuts, crackers, and salt. Place in 4 sherbet glasses. Top each with a cherry. Chill.

# Orange Ambrosia

Allow 1 medium-sized orange for each serving. Peel and slice. Arrange in layers in serving bowl or individual dishes with shredded or flaked coconut between layers and on top.

# Raspberry Macaroon Dessert

| | |
|---|---|
| 2 Tablespoons sherry, cream or dry | 1 10-ounce package quick-thaw frozen raspberries |
| 4 soft macaroons | 1 pint vanilla ice cream |

Sprinkle sherry over raspberries. Crumble one macaroon in each of 4 sherbet dishes. Top macaroons with a scoop of ice cream. Spoon raspberry mixture over top. If raspberries are at room temperature, entire dessert may be prepared and kept in the freezer during dinner.

# Apple Baked Alaska

| | |
|---|---|
| 4 cups sliced apples | 1/2 cup seedless raisins |
| 1/4 cup water | 1/2 cup firmly packed brown sugar |
| 1 teaspoon cinnamon | |
| 1/4 teaspoon mace | 3 egg whites |
| 1/8 teaspoon salt | 6 Tablespoons sugar |
| 1 pint firm vanilla or coffee ice cream | |

Combine apples and raisins in 1 1/2-quart baking dish. Sprinkle with water. Combine brown sugar, spices, and salt. Pour over apples. Bake at 350 degrees for 30 to 35 minutes or until apples are soft, stirring occasionally. Chill. Just before serving, beat egg whites until stiff. Add sugar gradually while continuing to beat until very stiff and glossy. Spoon ice cream over apples. Top with deep swirls of meringue, being careful to bring meringue to edge of dish. Bake in preheated oven at 450 degrees for 3 or 4 minutes or until meringue is tipped with brown. Makes 6 servings.

# Heavenly Hash Ice Cream Loaf

1 loaf angel food cake
1 pint heavy cream, whipped
1/4 cup nuts, chopped
1 10-ounce package frozen strawberries, drained

1 quart strawberry ice cream
1 cup miniature marshmallows
1 8-ounce can crushed pineapple, drained

Slice angel food cake lengthwise. Place a layer of strawberry ice cream 1 inch thick between cake slices, sandwich style. Make an icing of whipped cream to which marshmallows, nuts, pineapple and strawberries have been added; spread over entire cake. Keep in freezer until ready to serve. Loaf slices easily if sliced as soon as it is taken from the freezer.

# Lemon Ice Cream

1/2 pint cream or evaporated milk
pinch salt
1/2 cup sugar
grated lemon rind
3 Tablespoons sugar

1 Tablespoon sugar
orange or vanilla flavoring
3 egg yolks
juice of 2 lemons
3 egg whites
vanilla wafers, crushed

Whip cream or milk with 1 tablespoon sugar. Add flavoring and salt. Put in refrigerator. Gradually add the 1/2 cup of sugar to egg yolks as they are being beaten. Then add the lemon juice and grated rind, and cook, stirring constantly until thick. Cool. Next, beat the egg whites with the 3 tablespoons of sugar; add to the egg yolk mixture. Fold in whipped cream. Line pan with crushed vanilla wafers, pour in mixture, and sprinkle with more vanilla wafers. Freeze.

# Fresh Peach Ice Cream

During our early married years, Don and I lived in a little hamlet outside of Spartanburg, South Carolina. I had a small piano studio and among my students were two daughters of a peach orchard owner. This afforded us the opportunity to visit his peach sheds during harvest time to gather "culls," or castoffs. They made the very best, freshest peach ice cream I have ever eaten before or since. (The peach cobbler they made wasn't bad either.) M.P.

| | | | |
|---|---|---|---|
| 2 | cups sugar | 3 | eggs |
| 1 | teaspoon salt | 1 | cup evaporated milk |
| 1 | cup mashed fresh peaches | 1 | quart whole milk |

Beat sugar and eggs together. Add salt and evaporated milk. Pour into chilled ice cream freezer can. Add mashed peaches and whole milk. Freeze according to freezer directions.

*Iva Suttles, Spartanburg, South Carolina*

 # Lemon Sherbet

Ice cream was a good summer treat for the children, but making it was a time consuming process for granny.

| | | | |
|---|---|---|---|
| 3 | oranges | 3 | lemons, grated |
| 1 | can pineapple | 2 | cups sugar |
| 1 | envelope gelatin | 1 1/2 | egg whites |

Get out all juice; then boil lemon rinds in water. Take out rinds and put in sugar, and boil it. Fix the gelatin with this syrup. Let cool, and put in fruit and juice with it. Put in enough water to make freezer 2/3 full. When it starts to freeze, drop in egg whites -- unbeaten.

*Annie Harrell Stewart, Charlotte, North Carolina*

# Ice Cream — Uncooked — Basic Recipe

| | |
|---|---|
| 1/2 cup sugar | 2 Tablespoons sugar |
| 2 eggs | 1 cup whipping cream |
| 1 1/3 cups top milk or | dash salt |
| evaporated milk | 1 teaspoon vanilla |

Dissolve 1/2 cup sugar and salt in milk. Beat egg yolks until thick; add to milk and sugar. Beat egg whites until stiff; then beat in 2 tablespoons sugar. Beat cream until thick but not stiff. Stir all together gently. For plain ice cream, add 1 teaspoon vanilla. Stir once while freezing. Add any fruits, nuts, etc. desired. This is real good — rich — doesn't get so icy.

*Annie Harrell Stewart, Charlotte, North Carolina*

 # Tutti-Frutti

Heat to boiling point one pint of rich milk. Beat the yolks of two eggs very light, and stir into them the whites of six eggs, beat into a stiff froth. Add both to the boiling milk, stirring all the while. When thick, remove it from the fire and cool. Sweeten three pints of rich cream whipped to a froth and stir into cool mixture. Add the juice and grated peel of two lemons, six tablespoonfuls of sherry, and one pound of choicest candied fruits. Freeze.

 # English Christmas Plum Pudding

One pound of raisins, one pound of currants, one pound of suet, one pound of flour, six eggs, half a pound of brown sugar, one nutmeg, one pint of milk, one teaspoonful of salt; mix these ingredients thoroughly; place them in a strong pudding-cloth, which has been wet and covered with flour; tie up the cloth, not leaving much room for the pudding to swell. Serve with rich sauce after boiling five hours.

# Lemon Cake Pudding

| | |
|---|---|
| 1 cup sugar | 3 Tablespoons soft butter |
| 3 Tablespoons flour | 2 eggs, separated |
| juice and grated rind | 1 cup milk |
| of 1 lemon | |

Cream the sugar and butter. Add flour, beaten egg yolks, rind and lemon juice, and milk. Mix well, and fold in stiffly beaten egg whites. Pour into 1-quart casserole. Place casserole in pan of hot water; bake at 325 degrees for 1 hour until top surface is golden brown.

 # Puddings

The outside of a boiled pudding often tastes disagreeable, which comes by the cloth not being nicely washed, and kept in a dry place. It should be dipped in boiling water, squeezed dry, and floured when to be used. If bread it should be tied loose, if batter, tight over. The water should boil quick when the pudding is put in, and it should be moved about for a minute, lest the ingredients should not mix. A pan of cold water should be ready, and the pudding dipped in as soon as it comes out of the pot, and then it will not adhere to the cloth. Very good puddings may be made without eggs, but they must have as little milk as will mix, and must boil three or four hours. Batter pudding should be strained through a coarse sieve when all is mixed. In others, the eggs separately. The pans and basins must be always buttered for a baked pudding. A few spoonfuls of fresh small beer, or one of yeast, will answer instead of eggs. Snow is an excellent substitute for eggs, either in puddings or in pancakes. Two large spoonfuls will supply the place of eggs.

# Fudge Pudding

| | |
|---|---|
| 2 cups hot water | 6 Tablespoons cocoa |
| 2 teaspoons vanilla | 1 cup sugar |
| 1/2 teaspoon salt | 1 package fudge cake mix |

Bring water to boil in a saucepan. Add other ingredients; stir. Grease large glass dish, and pour cake mix into it. Pour sauce over mix. Bake at 375 degrees for 30 minutes.

# Apple Rice Pudding

| | |
|---|---|
| 1/3 cup rice | 1 teaspoon vanilla |
| 2 cups milk | 2 eggs, separated |
| 5 medium apples | butter or margarine |
| sugar | cinnamon |

Cook rice for 5 minutes. Drain. In a saucepan, combine vanilla, rice, and milk. Cook until all liquid has been absorbed. Add egg yolks to rice mixture. Peel, and slice apples; brown in butter or margarine. Grease baking dish, and spread rice in the bottom. Add apples to cover; sprinkle with cinnamon and sugar.

**Meringue:**
While beating 2 egg whites, gradually add 1/2 cup sugar until whites are stiff enough for meringue. Spread over apples; bake in 350 degree oven until lightly browned.

# Fruit Whip

Beat 2 egg whites until stiff. If needed, gradually beat in a little powdered sugar. Fold in 1 cup fruit pulp. (crushed berries, peaches, applesauce, prune, or apricot pulp) Pile in sherbet glasses; chill. Makes 4 servings.

# Baked Custard

| | | | |
|---|---|---|---|
| 2 | eggs | 2 | Tablespoons sugar |
| 3 or 4 | graham crackers | 8 or 10 | marshmallows |
| 1 1/2 | cups milk | | |

Heat milk, and pour over cracker crumbs. Add sugar to eggs. Add mixture to milk and crackers. Add marshmallows, and bake.

# Sherry Pudding

| | | | |
|---|---|---|---|
| 1 | package Knox gelatin | 1/2 | cup cold water |
| 6 | egg yolks | 1 | cup sherry |
| 1 | cup sugar | 6 | egg whites, beaten |
| 1 | cup vanilla wafers, crushed | 1 | cup pecans, finely chopped |

Dissolve gelatin in cold water. Combine egg yolks, sherry, and sugar, and cook in double boiler until thick. Add enough hot water to gelatin mixture to pour (2 or 3 drops); add to custard. Beat egg whites until stiff, and fold in. Grind vanilla wafers and pecans. In greased pan, put a layer of custard; then, a layer of the mix. Continue until all is used. Chill, and serve with whipped cream.

# Porcupine Pudding

Boil half a pint of rice in new milk until perfectly tender, and not too dry; then add six eggs beaten, a spoonful of ratafia, as much as sugar as shall be sufficient, and some grated fresh lemon; mix well, and boil in a mould one hour and a half. Turn it on a hot dish, and stick it thick with almonds cut in sixths. Serve with a rich custard around it. It is equally good cold. (Comment: Ratafia is an almond-flavored liqueur.)

# Bread Pudding with Lemon Sauce

| | |
|---|---|
| 1/4 cup sugar | 1/4 teaspoon salt |
| 1 teaspoon vanilla | 2 Tablespoons margarine, |
| 1/2 teaspoon cinnamon | melted |
| 1 egg | 2 cups milk, scalded |
| 1 cup bread cubes | 1/2 cup raisins |

Combine sugar, salt, vanilla, melted margarine, cinnamon, and slightly beaten egg. Slowly add scalded milk. Stirring constantly, add bread cubes and raisins. Mix thoroughly, and pour into buttered baking dish. Set in pan of warm water. Bake at 350 degrees for 1 hour.

**Sauce:**

| | |
|---|---|
| 1 1/2 Tablespoons corn starch | 1/4 cup sugar |
| 1 1/2 cups hot water | grated rind of 1 lemon |
| 2 Tablespoons lemon juice | 1 1/2 Tablespoons margarine |

Put corn starch and sugar in a saucepan. Slowly add hot water, stirring constantly. Add grated lemon rind. Cook over hot water until thickened. Remove from heat, and stir in lemon juice and margarine. Spoon sauce over bread pudding when served.

*"Sis" Proffitt, Salisbury, Maryland*

# Maple Parfait

| | |
|---|---|
| 5 eggs, separated | 1 pint cream |
| 1 cup maple syrup | |

Cook beaten egg yolks in double boiler with maple syrup until thick. Cool. Add beaten egg whites and cream. Freeze.

# Boiled Custard

| | |
|---|---|
| 1 quart milk | 6 rounded Tablespoons sugar |
| 2 rounded Tablespoons cornstarch | 2 eggs, well-beaten |
| 1 teaspoon vanilla | |

Heat milk until water in double boiler boils. Mix sugar and cornstarch, and add to milk. Stir until it begins to thicken. Add well-beaten eggs, and cook about ten minutes, stirring constantly. Pour into a warm bowl, stirring as you pour. When it cools, add the vanilla.

*Mary S. Moss, Washington, North Carolina*

# Apple Brown Betty

| | |
|---|---|
| 1 cup soft bread crumbs or ready-to-eat dry cereal | 3 Tablespoons butter or oleo |
| 1 teaspoon cinnamon | 1 teaspoon grated orange or lemon peel |
| 1/2 cup sugar | 4 medium apples, sliced |
| 1/4 cup fruit juice (approximately) | |

Preheat oven to 375 degrees. Mix bread crumbs, butter or oleo, lemon peel, sugar, and cinnamon. Place 1/2 of the apples in buttered baking dish. Cover with 1/2 of the bread crumb mixture. Add remaining apple slices; cover with remaining crumb mixture. Sprinkle with fruit juice. Bake about 45 minutes. Serve hot or cold with milk, cream, custard sauce, or other dessert sauce. Makes 6 servings.

**Variations:** With mincemeat, use 1/2 cup mincemeat and 3 apples.
With rhubarb, use 2 cups stewed sweetened rhubarb in place of apples. Omit sugar, cinnamon, and fruit juice.

# Baked Bananas

| | |
|---|---|
| 4  bananas | 4  Tablespoons sugar |
| 4  teaspoons hot water | 1  Tablespoon butter or oleo |

Peel bananas, and split in halves.  Place in shallow baking dish.  Melt butter in hot water; pour over bananas.  Sprinkle layer of bananas with a little cinnamon and/or lemon juice.  A little salt may be sprinkled on fruit also.  Bake at 350 degrees about 20 minutes or until brown.

 # Gretchen's Apple Dessert

| | |
|---|---|
| 1  egg, beaten | 1  cup sugar |
| 1  cup flour | 1  teaspoon baking powder |
|    salt | 1/2  teaspoon vanilla |
| 3  medium or 4 small apples | |

Combine ingredients, and bake in a moderate oven at least 1 hour.

# Banana Whip

| | |
|---|---|
| 6  medium bananas | 6  Tablespoons confectioners' |
| 1  Tablespoon lemon juice |    sugar |
| 1/2  teaspoon vanilla | 1/2  cup nuts, chopped |
| 4  egg whites, whipped | 1/8  teaspoon salt |

Mash the bananas through a ricer or food mill.  Beat in the sugar, lemon juice, vanilla, and nuts.  Whip the egg whites with the salt until stiff.  Fold them  into banana mixture.  Place in baking dish, and bake at 325 degrees for about 30 minutes.  Serve hot or cold.  Makes 6 servings.

# Delicious Dessert

| | |
|---|---|
| 1   cup yellow cake mix | 1/2   cup chopped nuts |
| 1/2   stick oleo, melted | 1   can cherry or apple pie filling |

Mix together the cake mix, nuts, and melted oleo.  Grease a shallow pan (larger than a pie tin).  Put in 1 can pie filling; put cake mix on top.  Bake in 350 degree oven about 30 to 40 minutes.  Crushed pineapple may be added to the cherries.  Serve with scoop of vanilla ice cream.

*Mary S. Moss, Washington, North Carolina*

# Peach Cobbler

| | |
|---|---|
| 15   medium peaches, sliced | 2   cups sugar |
| 1   Tablespoon lemon juice | 2   teaspoons ground ginger |
| 1/3   cup flour | 1   teaspoon salt |

Combine ingredients and mix.

**Pastry:**

| | |
|---|---|
| 3   cups sifted all-purpose flour | 2   teaspoons salt |
| 1   cup shortening | 1/2   cup water |

Combine flour and salt. Cut in shortening.  Sprinkle with water.  Press dough into a ball.  Roll out 1/3 of the dough and cut into thin strips.  Roll out rest of dough for top crust.  Pour half the peach filling into a buttered 9x12-inch baking dish.  Cover with pastry strips.  Add remaining filling.  Dot with 3 tablespoons of butter, and cover with top crust. Slit center of top crust several times.  Bake in 350 degree oven for 1 hour.  Makes 12 servings.

*Margaret Taylor Proffitt, Virginia Beach, Virginia*

# Pies

## Plain Pastry

When Mother made a pie and had a few pieces of dough left over, she would put a little butter and brown sugar on the pieces and cook them in the oven as a treat for my sister and me. Cinnamon and sugar mix substituted for brown sugar is also good. M.D.

| | |
|---|---|
| 1 1/4 cups sifted flour | 1 teaspoon salt |
| 1/2 cup shortening | 3 to 4 Tablespoons ice water |

Combine flour and salt; cut in shortening with pastry blender. Blend until mixture is crumbly. Sprinkle water. Mix lightly with fork until pastry holds together and leaves sides of bowl.

## Grandmother's Pastry

| | |
|---|---|
| 3 cups flour | 1 teaspoon salt |
| 1/2 pound lard (1 cup) | 1/2 cup boiling water |

Stir lard and water until creamy. Stir in flour and salt. Put in refrigerator. May be used at once or kept a week covered.

*Annie Harrell Stewart, Charlotte, North Carolina*

## Bubbling Pie

To prevent pies from bubbling over, insert a few pieces of macaroni through the crust. These do not affect the flavor and can be removed.

# Sour Cream Apple Pie

| | |
|---|---|
| 1/4  cup flour | 2  eggs |
| 1/2  teaspoon salt | 1 1/2  cups sour cream |
| 3/4  cups sugar | 1  teaspoon vanilla |
| 2  medium apples | 1  pie shell, unbaked |
| 1  teaspoon Real Lemon | |

Sift flour, sugar, and salt in a large bowl.  Add eggs, and beat well.  Add vanilla and sour cream; beat gently until smooth.  Peel apples, slice thin, mix with Real Lemon, and pour into pie shell.  Bake at 400 degrees for 10 minutes.  Remove from oven, and cover with Spicy Topping.  Return to oven. Bake for 30 to 35 minutes until firm.  Cool and refrigerate.

**Spicy Topping:**

| | |
|---|---|
| 1/3  cup brown sugar | 1/3  cup flour |
| 1/2  teaspoon cinnamon | 1/4  cup margarine |

Combine sugar, flour, and cinnamon.  Cut in margarine to make a coarse mixture.  Spread over pie.

*Janie Proffitt Flippo, Roanoke, Virginia*

# Caramel Pie

| | |
|---|---|
| 1  cup milk | 2  Tablespoons flour |
| 2  eggs, separated | 1  cup brown sugar |
| 1  teaspoon butter | 1  teaspoon vanilla |
| 1  baked pie shell | |

Scald milk in top of double boiler.  In a bowl, mix flour, yolks of eggs, sugar, and scalded milk. Cook in double boiler until thick.  Add butter and vanilla. Pour into baked pie shell.  Make meringue of egg whites, spread over top of pie.  Bake until brown.

# Quick Apple Pie

2 frozen deep dish pie crusts
2 Tablespoons lemon juice
3/4 cup sugar
1 teaspoon cinnamon
1/4 cup water

5 or 6 medium apples, peeled
and sliced
2 Tablespoons cornstarch
1 teaspoon nutmeg
3 teaspoons butter

Thaw pie crust while slicing apples. Sprinkle lemon juice over apples. In another bowl, mix cornstarch with sugar and spices. Add water, and mix well. Pour over apples. Mix well. Spoon into one of the pie crusts. Dot with butter. Turn the other pie crust upside down on top of the apples. Crimp edges together, and make holes in top of crust with fork. Bake in 350 degree oven approximately 1 hour.

# Strawberry Pie

Picking strawberries in Virginia Beach is a great way to introduce children and grandchildren to one type of farming. They learn about hard work and also grow to appreciate the wonderful, fresh taste of anything gathered, prepared, and eaten right at home. When they were very young, strawberry pie was one of our sons' favorites because the recipe came from their first grade teacher. They got a fine start in their education at Lynnhaven Elementary School under the caring eye of Marguerite Brassell. She was a gem of a teacher and, though no longer living in the area, remains a good friend. M.P.

3 Tablespoons strawberry jello
1 cup sugar
fresh strawberries

3 Tablespoons cornstarch
Cool Whip, or ice cream
1 cup water

Mix dry ingredients together in a saucepan. Add water, bring to a boil, and cook until thick. Cool. Add berries, and pour into a baked pie shell. Place in refrigerator until chilled and firm. Add your favorite topping.

*Marguerite Brassell, Dover, Delaware*

# Cranberry Pie

Hired on just 24 hours notice, Emily Groover Shelley, more famously known as "Mama Groover," quickly became the supreme chef and cafeteria manager at Lynnhaven Elementary School when it opened in 1963. The children were always happy to hear her announce over the P.A. system that the next day's menu would include Mama Groover's Round Pizza. In the days when lots of government surplus food was sent to the schools — often on short notice — Emily rapidly and cleverly incorporated the products into delicious fare. Mary and I recall with amazement and amusement the numerous ways in which she worked her wizardry with the seemingly endless supply of cranberries that arrived unexpectedly. The recipe shared here is from a recipe book put together by the happy faculty at that special school. M. P.

| | | | |
|---|---|---|---|
| 2 | cups cranberries | 1/2 | cup sugar |
| 1/2 | cup nuts | 1/2 | cup butter |
| 1/2 | cup Crisco | 1/4 | cup oil |
| 2 | eggs | 1 | cup sugar |
| 1 | cup flour | | |

Wash, pick over, and drain 2 cups of cranberries. Put in bottom of a large pie pan. Sprinkle 1/2 cup of sugar over cranberries; then sprinkle on nuts. Set aside. Melt together butter, Crisco, and oil. Beat 2 eggs thoroughly with 1 cup sugar; add flour, and mix well. Combine both mixtures, and pour over cranberries. Bake 1 hour or until golden brown. Serve warm. Delicious topped with ice cream.

# Juicy Oranges

To peel oranges more easily, place them in boiling water for 3 or 4 minutes. This also makes them more juicy.

# Aunt V.'s Lemon Pie

| | |
|---|---|
| 1 cup flour | 1/4 teaspoon salt |
| lard (size of an egg) | ice water |

To make crust, work flour and lard together. Add salt and ice water (just enough to make it stick). Handle as little as possible so it will be light. Roll out and put in pie pan. Prick edges with fork. Cool it, then bake.

**Filling:**

| | |
|---|---|
| 1 cup sugar | 2 round Tablespoons flour |
| 1 cup hot water | 1 small lump butter |
| 3 eggs, separated | 1 large lemon, juice only |
| 1/2 teaspoon grated lemon rind | dash of salt |

Combine sugar and flour. Add salt, egg yolks, lemon juice, and rind. Mix. Add hot water and butter. Cook in double boiler until thick (about 5 or 10 minutes). Put the filling in baked pie crust. Top with meringue in swirls.

**Meringue:**

| | |
|---|---|
| 3 egg whites | 3 Tablespoons sugar |
| 1/2 teaspoon baking powder | a little lemon juice |

Beat egg whites until stiff. Add baking powder, sugar, and lemon juice.

# Pineapple Coconut Pie

Mix one stick melted margarine, two tablespoons flour, and one and three-quarters cups of sugar. Add four slightly beaten eggs, one small can undrained crushed pineapple, one cup coconut, one teaspoon lemon extract, and one teaspoon vanilla extract. Pour into two unbaked pie shells and bake at 350 degrees for 35 minutes.

# Lemon Pie

This collection of recipes would not be complete without my mother's lemon pie recipe. It has always been a favorite. Mother must have had a special touch, because mine are never quite the same as the ones she made for us. M.D.

| | | | |
|---|---|---|---|
| 1 | can condensed milk | 2 | Tablespoons sugar |
| 3 | lemons (juice) | | 2 egg whites, beaten |
| | graham crackers | | |

Mix lemon juice and milk. Roll crackers, and spread in bottom of Pyrex pie pan. Place broken graham crackers around rim. Add filling. Cover with meringue made from egg whites and sugar. Bake in slow oven until it is brown. Chill.

*Mary S. Moss, Washington, North Carolina*

# Peach Custard Pie

| | | | |
|---|---|---|---|
| 5 | small or 4 large, ripe peaches | 3 | Tablespoons Gold Medal flour |
| 3 | Tablespoons brown sugar | | |
| 1 1/2 | cups evaporated milk (undiluted) | 1 | egg, slightly beaten |
| | | 2/3 | cup sugar |
| 2 | Tablespoons flour | 1/2 | teaspoon cinnamon |
| 1/4 | teaspoon nutmeg | | |

Make crust for a 9-inch one-crust pie (with high fluted edges). Peel peaches, and cut in half. Mix the brown sugar and 3 tablespoons of flour; sprinkle over pastry in pie pan. Arrange the peaches cut-side up on top of sugar mixture. Mix milk, egg, sugar, cinnamon, nutmeg, and 2 tablespoons flour together, and sprinkle over top of peaches. Bake 40 to 50 minutes in a hot oven (425 degrees) until a silver knife inserted 1 inch from the pastry edge comes out clean.

*Josephine Proffitt Clements, Lynchburg, Virginia*

# Orange Pie

Aunt Bebe lived and worked in Washington, D.C. for most of her adult life. After her retirement, she traveled many places with senior groups and played bridge whenever she could. She is now 92 years old and resides in Salisbury, Maryland, where my husband's brother Ike and his wife "Sis" take good care of her. She really enjoys a good joke, likes to go out to eat, and loves it when my husband takes her something he has prepared from the recipe collection she gave him when she moved into a retirement residence. This orange pie is a dessert she loved to make when it was time for the bridge party to be held at her house. M.P.

| | | | |
|---|---|---|---|
| 1 | peeled orange | 2 | egg yolks |
| 1 | cup sugar | 1 | cup milk |
| 1 | Tablespoon flour | 2 | egg whites |
| 2 | Tablespoons sugar | 1 | pie shell (graham cracker) |

Cut peeled orange into small pieces. Add egg yolks, sugar, milk, and flour. Mix well. Pour into prepared pie shell. Bake in 350 degree oven until set. Beat egg whites with sugar for meringue. Spread over pie; brown in oven.

*Genevieve Proffitt, Salisbury, Maryland*

# Hershey Bar Pie

This is from my friend who loves chocolate as much as I do! M.D.

| | | | |
|---|---|---|---|
| 6 | Hershey bars with almonds | 1/2 | cup milk |
| 16 | marshmallows | 1 | cup whipping cream |
| 1 | pie crust, baked | | |

Melt chocolate bars and marshmallows in milk. Set aside to cool. Whip the whipping cream, and fold into this mixture. Pour into baked pie crust which is thoroughly cooled. Refrigerate or freeze.

*Sherry Arendt, Virginia Beach, Virginia*

# German Chocolate Pie

| | | | |
|---|---|---|---|
| 1 | cup sugar | 2 | Tablespoons flour |
| 1 | Tablespoon cornstarch | | pinch of salt |
| 2 | Tablespoons cocoa | 2 | eggs |
| 3 | Tablespoons melted margarine | 2/3 | cup milk |
| 1 | teaspoon vanilla | 3/4 | cup coconut |
| 1/3 | cup pecan pieces | 1 | unbaked pie shell |

Melt oleo, and mix with remaining ingredients. Bake in preheated 400 degree oven.

*Janie Proffitt Flippo, Roanoke, Virginia*

# Chocolate Nut Pie

This is for our friends who REALLY love chocolate! M.D.

| | | | |
|---|---|---|---|
| 2 | unbaked pie shells | 1 | Tablespoon flour |
| 1 | cup sugar | 1 | cup chocolate chips |
| 4 | eggs, slightly beaten | 1 | cup light corn syrup |
| 1 | stick butter | 1 | cup pecans, finely chopped |

Combine flour and sugar. Add remaining ingredients; mix well. Pour mixture into pie shells. Bake at 350 degrees for 35 to 40 minutes. Good served with vanilla ice cream. You can divide the ingredients by half and make 1 pie.

# Impossible Pie

Makes 2 pies *and* own crusts. Cream one and three-quarters cups sugar with one-half cup self-rising flour. Add four well-beaten eggs, one-half stick melted butter or margarine, one teaspoon vanilla, two cups milk, and seven ounces flaked coconut. Pour into two nine-inch pie pans. Bake at 350 degrees for about 35 minutes or until brown on top.

# Chocolate Pie

3 eggs, separated
1 cup milk
1 Tablespoon flour
1 teaspoon vanilla

1 cup sugar
2 Tablespoons cocoa
1 teaspoon butter
pastry shell

Bake the pastry shell. Mix sugar, flour, and cocoa. Add to well-beaten egg yolks. Add milk and butter. Cook in double boiler until thick. Stir in vanilla. Pour into baked pie shell, and cover with stiffly beaten egg whites. Place in preheated oven; let meringue lightly brown.

# Presbyterian Chocolate Chess Pie

1 9-inch pie shell, unbaked
2 eggs
1 stick butter
dash salt

1 square of chocolate
2 teaspoons vanilla
1 cup sugar

Melt butter and chocolate. Blend remaining ingredients, and mix with butter and chocolate. Pour into unbaked pie shell. Bake at 350 degrees for 30 minutes. Serves 6.

*Mary S. Moss, Washington, North Carolina*

 # Chess Cake

2 1/2 cups sugar
4 eggs
vanilla flavoring

1 cup butter
1 cup milk
pinch of salt

Cream butter and sugar, add eggs beaten lightly, then milk. Pour mixture into 2 unbaked pie shells. Bake slowly until brown.

# Pecan Pie

| | |
|---|---|
| 1 cup pecans | 2 eggs, well beaten |
| pinch of salt | 1 teaspoon vanilla |
| 3 Tablespoons melted butter | 1 cup dark Karo syrup |
| 1 cup brown sugar | pie shell |

Mix sugar, Karo syrup, eggs, salt, vanilla, and melted butter. Put in unbaked pie shell. Stir in nuts; put some nuts on top. Bake in a 350 degree oven for 30 to 40 minutes or until firm.

*Mary S. Moss, Washington, North Carolina*

# Pecan Molasses Pie

| | |
|---|---|
| 1/2 cup sugar | 2 Tablespoons butter |
| 2 eggs | 2 Tablespoons flour |
| 1/4 Tablespoon salt | 1 teaspoon almond extract |
| 1 cup white Karo syrup | 1 1/2 cups pecans, chopped |

Cream butter and sugar. Add beaten eggs, flour, salt, almond extract, and syrup. Stir well. Add pecan pieces, and pour into a crust. Bake 1/2 hour in a moderate oven.

*Annie Harrell Stewart, Charlotte, North Carolina*

# Rum Pie

| | |
|---|---|
| 1 large Cool Whip | 1 8-ounce Hershey's chocolate |
| 4 Tablespoons rum, light | bar, plain |
| 2 graham cracker pie crusts | |

Thaw Cool Whip. Melt chocolate over hot water; mix with Cool Whip. Add rum, and stir. Pour into pie crusts. Freeze

# Georgia Pecan Pie

| | | | |
|---|---|---|---|
| 1/2 | cup softened butter or margarine | 1 | cup sugar |
| 1 | cup firmly packed brown sugar | 2 | Tablespoons all-purpose flour |
| 3/4 | cup milk | 3 | eggs, beaten |
| 1 | teaspoon vanilla | 1 1/2 | cups chopped pecans |
| | | 1 | unbaked pie shell |

Cream together melted butter and sugars. Add flour, eggs, and milk. Beat together thoroughly. Stir in pecans and vanilla. Pour into unbaked pie shell. Bake in 350 degree oven for 1 hour.

*Janie Proffitt Flippo, Roanoke, Virginia*

# Derby Tarts

| | | | |
|---|---|---|---|
| 2 | eggs | 1 | cup sugar |
| 1/4 | cup butter or margarine, melted | 2 | Tablespoons bourbon |
| 1/2 | teaspoon vanilla extract | 1/2 | cup all-purpose flour |
| 1/2 | cup semisweet chocolate morsels, melted powdered sugar | 1/2 | cup chopped pecans |
| 10 | pecan halves | 10 | 3-inch pastry shells, unbaked whipped cream |

Beat eggs just until blended. Gradually add sugar, beating until thick and light colored. Add butter, bourbon, and vanilla. Mix well. Gradually add flour, beating well. Stir in chocolate and chopped pecans. Spoon 1/4 cup filling into each pastry shell. Bake at 350 degrees for 30 minutes. Cool tarts completely. Sift powdered sugar lightly over tarts. Top with a dollop of whipped cream, and garnish each with a pecan half.

*Sara S. Gabel, Washington, North Carolina*

# Sweet Potato Pecan Pie

| | |
|---|---|
| 1/4 cup butter | 1/2 cup brown sugar |
| 1 cup mashed sweet potatoes | 3 eggs |
| 1/3 cup corn syrup | 1/3 cup milk |
| 1/2 teaspoon salt | 1 teaspoon vanilla |
| 1 cup broken pecan pieces | pastry shell |

Cream together butter and sugar. Add potatoes and slightly beaten eggs. Mix well, and combine with syrup, milk, salt, vanilla, and pecans. Pour into unbaked pastry shell. Bake at 425 degrees for 10 minutes. Reduce heat to 325 degrees; bake 35 to 45 minutes longer. If you do not use pecans, increase sweet potatoes to 1 1/2 cups.

# Sweet Potato Pie

| | |
|---|---|
| 4 eggs | 1 1/2 cups sweet potatoes |
| 1/3 cup sugar | 2/3 cup milk |
| 1/2 cup walnuts or pecans, finely chopped | 1/3 cup orange juice |
| 1 teaspoon vanilla | 2 Tablespoons honey |
| 1 Tablespoon grated orange peel | 1/2 teaspoon nutmeg |
| | unbaked pie shell |

Beat eggs until very light. Beat in the cooked and mashed sweet potatoes and sugar. Stir in the milk, nuts, orange juice, honey, and vanilla. Pour into pie shell. Bake in 450 degree oven for 10 minutes. Reduce temperature to 350 degrees; bake 30 minutes longer or until knife inserted near center comes out clean. Cool. Spread with whipped cream flavored with grated orange peel and nutmeg.

*Mary S. Moss, Washington, North Carolina*

# Buttermilk Pie

| | |
|---|---|
| 3 cups sugar | 1/2 cup melted butter |
| 1/2 cup flour | 3 eggs, beaten |
| 1/2 teaspoon soda | 1 teaspoon vanilla flavoring |
| 2 cups buttermilk | 1 teaspoon lemon flavoring |
| 2 unbaked pie shells | |

Sift together sugar, flour, soda. Add beaten eggs, milk, and melted butter. Stir in lemon and vanilla flavorings. Pour into unbaked pie shells. Bake for 10 to 15 minutes in 450 degree oven. Turn oven down to 325 degrees; continue baking for 20 to 25 minutes.

*Janie Proffitt Flippo, Roanoke, Virginia*

 # Squash Pie

Pare the squash and remove the seeds; stew until soft and dry; then pulp it through a colander. Stir into the pulp enough sweet milk to make it thick as batter. Spice with ginger, cinnamon, nutmeg or other seasoning to taste; sweeten with sugar and add four beaten eggs for each quart of milk. Fill a pie plate lined with crust and bake one hour.

# Chess Pies

| | |
|---|---|
| 1/2 cup butter | 2 teaspoons vanilla |
| 1 cup sugar | 1 cup chopped dates |
| 2 eggs, beaten | 1/2 cup chopped nuts |

Cream butter until soft. Add the sugar, and beat until creamy. Add the eggs, and beat well. Add the rest of the ingredients. Mix. Pour into muffin pans which have been lined with pastry. Bake for 30 minutes in a moderate oven. Serve cold, topped with whipped cream. These are very rich.

*Annie Harrell Stewart, Charlotte, North Carolina*

# Vinegar Pie

| | |
|---|---|
| 1/2 cup butter | 1 cup sugar |
| 2 eggs | 4 teaspoons vinegar |
| 1 teaspoon vanilla | 1 cup nuts, chopped |
| pinch of salt | 1 unbaked pie shell |

Melt butter. Add sugar and salt. Beat until creamy. Add eggs, and beat some more. Add vanilla and vinegar. Mix. Add nuts, and pour into unbaked pie shell. Bake at 325 degrees about 30 minutes. Test with toothpick or straw as you would a cake.

*Mary S. Moss, Washington, North Carolina*

# Grasshopper Pie

| | |
|---|---|
| 1 1/2 cups chocolate wafer crumbs | 1/4 cup melted butter |
| | 4 cups miniature marshmallows |
| 1/2 cup milk | 1/4 cup white creme de cacao |
| 1/4 cup green creme de menthe | 2 cups whipping cream |
| chocolate curls for garnish | |

Combine wafer crumbs and butter in medium bowl; mix well. Press into bottom and sides of 9-inch pie plate. Cook in 500 degree oven for about 3 minutes. Cool slightly. Refrigerate. Combine marshmallows and milk in top of double boiler. Stir and leave over heat until marshmallows begin to melt. After they have melted completely, let them cool slightly. Blend in creme de cacao and creme de menthe. Let cool completely. Fold in all but 1/2 cup of the whipped cream. Spoon mixture into prepared crust. Garnish with remaining whipped cream, and sprinkle with chocolate curls or grated chocolate. Refrigerate until firm. Serve chilled.

# Crumb Pie (Cracker Cake)

| | |
|---|---|
| 1 cup Uneeda biscuits | 2 eggs |
| 1 cup sugar | 1 cup nuts, chopped |
| 1 teaspoon almond extract | 1 teaspoon baking powder |

In a bowl, break biscuits into coarse crumbs. Add beaten eggs and other ingredients. Put in Pyrex pie plate that has been greased and floured. Bake 35 minutes in 275 degree (slow) oven. Serve with whipped cream or ice cream.

*Mary S. Moss, Washington, North Carolina*

# Ritz Cracker Pie

| | |
|---|---|
| 3 egg whites | 1 cup sugar |
| 20 Ritz crackers, finely crushed | 1 Tablespoon baking powder |
| 3/4 cup nuts, chopped | |

Beat egg whites until stiff. Fold in sugar mixed with baking powder, Ritz crackers, and nuts. Put into a well-greased 9-inch pie plate. Bake at 350 degrees for 25 minutes. Cool. Serve with whipped cream or ice cream.

*Mary S. Moss, Washington, North Carolina*

# Chocolate Silk Pie

| | |
|---|---|
| 1 cup sugar | 1 cup butter |
| 3 squares unsweetened chocolate, melted | 1 teaspoon vanilla |
| 1 10-inch pie crust | 4 eggs |
| | whipped cream |

Cream butter and sugar. Add chocolate, vanilla, and 2 eggs. Beat at high speed for 5 minutes. Add 2 eggs; beat 5 minutes. Pour into pie crust. Chill overnight. Top with whipped cream.

# Macaroon Pie

| 16 | saltines, finely rolled | 16 | pitted dates, finely chopped |
| 1/2 | cup pecans, chopped | 1 | cup sugar |
| 1/4 | teaspoon baking powder | 3 | egg whites |

Blend saltines, dates, pecans, and sugar. Add baking powder to egg whites, and beat until stiff but not dry. Fold egg whites into saltine mixture; spread in well-buttered 9-inch pie plate. Bake at 350 degrees for 30 minutes. Cool. Serve topped with whipped cream or ice cream. To make miniature pies, spoon mixture into 18 aluminum foil miniature baking cups or use paper cups in miniature muffin tins. Bake at 350 degrees about 25 minutes. Cool, and serve in baking cups.

# Michael's Mud Pie

| 1 | chocolate pie crust | 2 | pints coffee ice cream |
| | whipped cream or Cool Whip | 1 | 12-ounce jar Smucker's |
| | sliced almonds | | Chocolate Fudge Topping |

Soften ice cream in refrigerator. Spoon into bowl, stirring until ice cream is just pliable. Spoon into pie crust, cover with inverted plastic lid, and place in freezer until hard. Cover with topping, and freeze again. Cut into wedges. Top each wedge with whipped cream or Cool Whip and sliced almonds.

*Sara S. Gabel, Washington, North Carolina*

# Crumb Crust

Preheat oven to 400 degrees. Mix one and one-half cups graham cracker crumbs with one-quarter cup of sugar and one-quarter cup butter or margarine. Lightly grease 9-inch pie plate. Press mixture firmly and evenly against sides and bottom of plate. Bake 10 minutes. Cool; fill with favorite filling.

# Chocolate Ice-Box Pie

| | | | |
|---|---|---|---|
| 2 | squares unsweetened chocolate | 1 | stick butter |
| | | 1/4 | cup self-rising flour |
| 3/4 | cup sugar | 1 | teaspoon vanilla |
| 2 | eggs | 1 | 8-inch pie crust |

Melt chocolate and butter in double boiler. Cool. Mix sugar and flour. Add eggs one at a time, beating after each addition. Stir in vanilla. Combine egg mixture with chocolate mixture; pour into 8-inch pie crust. Bake in a 350 degree oven for 25 minutes. Store in refrigerator.

# Ambrosia Pie

| | | | |
|---|---|---|---|
| 1 | 3 1/4-ounce package vanilla pudding and pie filling | 1 | 3-ounce package orange-banana gelatin |
| 2 1/2 | cups water | | prepared whipped topping mix |

Combine pie filling mix, gelatin, and water in a saucepan. Cook, and stir over medium heat until mixture comes to a full boil and is thick and clear. Remove from heat. Chill until mixture begins to set. Prepare whipped topping mix according to directions. Thoroughly blend into the chilled pudding mixture. Spoon into Unbaked Coconut Crust. (See recipe below.) Chill until firm, at least 3 hours. Garnish with large puff of whipped topping and a sunburst arrangement of orange sections.

**Unbaked Coconut Crust:**

| | | | |
|---|---|---|---|
| 1/4 | cup butter | 2 | cups flaked coconut |

Melt butter in a skillet. Add coconut and sauté, stirring constantly until coconut is golden brown. Sprinkle mixture into a 9-inch pie pan, pressing firmly to cover bottom and sides. Cool to room temperature. (About 30 minutes.)

# Mile-High Strawberry Pie

Make at least 1 day ahead.

1 cup sugar
1 10-ounce package frozen
strawberries, partially thawed
pinch of salt
1 9-inch pastry shell or crumb
crust

2 egg whites
1 teaspoon vanilla
1 Tablespoon lemon juice
1 cup heavy cream or
whipping cream

Combine sugar, egg whites, strawberries, vanilla, lemon juice, and salt in large mixing bowl. Beat mixture at high speed for 15 minutes until thick, fluffy, and voluminous. Fold in whipped cream, and pile into baked pie crust. Freeze for several hours. After pie is frozen, wrap well in foil or plastic wrap. May be frozen up to 3 weeks. Slice, and serve immediately upon removal from freezer. 8 servings.

# Baked Banana Pie

3 eggs
1/4 cup sugar
1/4 teaspoon nutmeg, ground
whipped cream
1 8-inch pie crust

3/4 cup milk
1/4 cup all-purpose flour
4 ripe bananas, mashed
(1 1/3 cups)

In bowl, beat together eggs, milk, sugar, flour, and nutmeg just until smooth. Stir in mashed banana. Turn into buttered 8-inch pie plate. Sprinkle with additional nutmeg if desired. Bake in a 350 degree oven for 35 minutes or until knife inserted just off center comes out clean. Cool; then chill. Top wedges with whipped cream if desired.

# Blueberry Pie

| | |
|---|---|
| 1 stick oleo | 1/2 cup nuts, chopped |
| 1 cup flour | 1 can pie blueberries |
| 1/2 cup light brown sugar | 1 large Cool Whip |

Mix the oleo, flour, brown sugar, and nuts together. Spread in flat pan, and cook in the oven until lightly browned. Cool, and crumble. Put some of the crumbles in the bottoms of 2 pie pans. Spread with Cool Whip. Spread the blueberries over the top. Sprinkle remaining crumbles on top. Refrigerate. Makes 2 pies.

*Sara S. Gabel, Washington, North Carolina*

# Frosty Lemon Blueberry Pie

| | |
|---|---|
| 1 No. 2 can blueberry pie filling | 1 Tablespoon grated lemon peel |
| 1 pint lemon sherbet | 18 lemon flavored wafers |

Line bottom and sides of a 9-inch pie plate with lemon-flavored wafers. Combine pie filling and grated lemon peel. Turn into wafer-lined pie plate, and freeze. Spoon lemon sherbet over frozen blueberry mixture. Keep frozen until serving time.

# Funeral Tart Filling

This pie was often taken to the homes of friends when there was a death in their family. M.D.

Beat 4 eggs until light. Melt 1 stick of butter, and add eggs, 2 cups sugar, and juice of 3 lemons. A little grated lemon rind may be added. Cook in a double boiler until thick. Refrigerate. Use baked tart or pie shells.

# Mrs. Reid's Pie

This recipe came to Janie from Mrs. Ethel Reed (correct spelling) of Oriskany, Virginia. We don't know who the original Mrs. Reid was, but her pie sure is good. M.P.

1   can Eagle Brand Milk
1   No. 2 can crushed pineapple
1   small bag pecan pieces
2   graham cracker pie crusts

juice of 1 lemon
1   12-ounce container Cool Whip
1   can peaches, if desired

Mix milk and lemon juice. Add well-drained pineapple (and cut up peaches if desired). Fold in Cool Whip and nuts. Fill pie crusts, and cover with inverted plastic tops. Crimp the edges of the pie pan over the plastic top to seal. Store in refrigerator or freeze.

*Janie Proffitt Flippo, Roanoke, Virginia*

# Lemon Pie

1/4   pound butter
4   eggs
pinch of salt
1/4   cup hot water

1   pound sugar
3   lemons
1   package gelatin
2   prepared pie crusts

Melt butter in double boiler. Add in order: sugar and eggs, along with the juice and grated rind of lemons. Cook, stirring frequently, until thick. Dissolve gelatin in hot water, and stir into egg mixture. Pour into pie crusts. Cool. Top with whipped cream when served.

# Frozen Lemon Pie

| | | | |
|---|---|---|---|
| 3 | egg yolks | 1 | cup sugar |
| 1 | teaspoon grated lemon rind | 1/4 | cup lemon juice |
| 1 | cup whipping cream | | dash salt |
| 6 | zwieback crackers or vanilla wafers, crushed | 3 | egg whites |

Combine beaten egg yolks, sugar, lemon juice, lemon rind, and salt. Cook in double boiler until thick. Remove from heat, and cool. Beat egg whites until stiff; combine with whipped cream. Fold into custard mixture. Place half of the zwieback crumbs on bottom of dish, pour in lemon mixture, and sprinkle other half of crumbs on top. Freeze for 3 hours or longer. Vanilla wafers may be used instead of zwieback.

# Peanut Butter Ice Cream Pie

This is a great dessert because you can take one of the pies to a get-together of friends and privately enjoy knowing that you have another at home to munch on when the sweet tooth attacks. M.P.

| | | | |
|---|---|---|---|
| 1 | quart vanilla ice cream | 1 | small jar crunchy peanut butter |
| 1 | 8-ounce container Cool Whip | | |
| 2 | 8-inch chocolate crusts | | |

Allow ice cream to soften for 15 to 20 minutes. Mix well with peanut butter. Fold in Cool Whip. Pour into pie crusts, and freeze. Garnish with grated chocolate or chocolate curls. Makes 2 pies.

*Meg Heckel, Virginia Beach, Virginia*

# Sweet Syrups and Sauces

## Peanut Butter Sauce

2/3  cup evaporated milk
1/4  cup light corn syrup

1/2  cup peanut butter

Add evaporated milk to peanut butter a little at a time.  Blend until smooth.
Stir in corn syrup.  Makes 1 1/3 cups sauce.  Good spooned over chocolate
cake.

 ## Wine Sauce

A teacupful of sugar, with butter the size of an egg worked into it; add half a
teacupful of boiling water, and set it over a kettle of boiling water ten minutes;
just before going to the table, add a wine glass of wine and whites of two eggs
whipped to a froth.  Nutmeg or other flavoring may be used instead of the
wine, if preferred.

 ## Brown Sugar Sauce

2  cups brown sugar
1/2  teaspoon salt

2  Tablespoons butter
1/2  cup milk

Boil together, stirring constantly.  Use on gingerbread, pound cake, or ice
cream.

# Cocoa Syrup

1/2 pound cocoa          2 glasses water
2 pounds sugar

Add sugar to boiling water as it boils. Add cocoa gradually, and boil for ten minutes. Cool. Put in glass jar. Keep in a cool place.

# Chocolate Sauce

5 squares Baker's chocolate          1 stick butter
3 cups confectioners' sugar          1 14 1/2-ounce can evapo-
1 teaspoon vanilla                      rated milk

Melt butter and chocolate in heavy saucepan. Add milk and sugar alternately. Bring to a boil, stirring constantly, and cook about 5 minutes. Mixture should be thick and creamy. Remove from heat; stir in vanilla. Serve warm over ice cream or cake. Makes about 18 servings.

*Mary S. Moss, Washington, North Carolina*

# Hard Sauce

1/3 cup butter or margarine          1 cup confectioners' sugar
1 teaspoon vanilla

Cream butter or margarine until very soft. Sift confectioners' sugar, and gradually beat into butter. Cream until fluffy. Add vanilla to mixture; blend thoroughly. Chill.

# Lemon Sauce

| | | | |
|---|---|---|---|
| 2 | Tablespoons cornstarch | 1 | cup sugar |
| 2 | teaspoons grated lemon peel | 2 | cups water |
| 1/4 | cup lemon juice | 1/4 | cup butter or margarine |
| 1/4 | teaspoon salt | | |

In a saucepan, combine cornstarch, sugar, and lemon peel. Slowly add water. Cook over medium heat, stirring constantly until thickened. Remove from heat and add remaining ingredients, stirring gently until butter is melted and all ingredients are blended.

# Nutty  Chocolate Sauce

| | | | |
|---|---|---|---|
| 1 | square Baker's chocolate | 1 | Tablespoon butter |
| 2 | Tablespoons white syrup | 1 to 2 | cups boiling water |
| 1 | cup sugar | 1 | teaspoon vanilla |
| 1/2 | cup chopped nuts | | |

Melt chocolate with butter. Add other ingredients and cook about 5 minutes. The longer it cooks, the thicker it gets. Add a little water if it gets too thick. Chopped nuts may also be added.

 # Whipping Cream

If cream does not whip well, add a few drops of lemon juice.

# Vegetables and Side Dishes

## River Scene

*The coasts of Virginia and North Carolina have wonderful beaches, but equally beautiful are the meandering rivers and streams that wend their ways to the seashore. — M.P.*

# VEGETABLES AND SIDE DISHES

In Washington, North Carolina, where I grew up, the farmers' market, called
The Curb Market, was located in the basement of the Agriculture Building.
This is where the local farmers in Beaufort County would bring their produce
to sell on Saturday mornings. Mother would go early to get vegetables, and,
by the middle of the morning, she would have fresh vegetables cooking on the
stove. This is when I learned about preparing and cooking fresh vegetables,
though I must admit I don't have the instinct that Mother had. She always
knew exactly how much seasoning to use. It was an extra special treat when
Mother cooked fresh fish and cornbread to have with the vegetables!

My grandparents lived on Elizabeth Avenue in Charlotte, North Carolina. We
spent many summers visiting there. The back yard had room for a garden —
not an enormous garden — but a wonderful garden with rows of corn, beans,
cucumbers, tomatoes, and other vegetables. As a young child, I especially
liked the cherry tomatoes that grew in the garden. My grandfather would tell
me they were "volunteer" tomatoes because they were not planted, but grew
by themselves. M.D.

## Canned Beans

Blanch beans for 10 minutes. Pack in jars, not too tight. Put 1 teaspoon of
salt to each quart; fill with warm water, lay on lids, set in boiler of warm water,
and boil 1 hour and 20 minutes after reaching boiling point. Refill if necessary
with boiling water. Just before taking off, put on rubbers and put 2 teaspoons
of boiling vinegar to each quart. When you want to use them, put a pinch of
soda and 1 teaspoon of sugar and cook till done.

*Annie Harrell Stewart, Charlotte, North Carolina*

# Easy Baked Beans

| | | | |
|---|---|---|---|
| 1 | 31-ounce can pork and beans | 1 | Tablespoon prepared mustard |
| 1 | Tablespoon onion, minced | 1/2 | green pepper, diced |
| 1/2 | cup brown sugar | 3 | Tablespoons liquid smoke |
| 1/4 | teaspoon salt | | dash Worcestershire sauce |
| 3 | Tablespoons catsup | 1/3 | cup molasses or brown |
| 3 | strips bacon, cooked and crumbled | | sugar |

Combine all ingredients and bake uncovered in a 350 degree oven for 1 hour.

# Broccoli Casserole

| | | | |
|---|---|---|---|
| 2 | packages frozen broccoli | 1 | can cream of chicken soup |
| 1/2 | cup Miracle Whip salad dressing | 1/2 | package Pepperidge Farm dry stuffing mix |
| 1/2 | cup butter (not margarine) | | |

Place cooked broccoli in a casserole. Mix the salad dressing and soup together; pour over broccoli. Top with stuffing crumbs. Pour the melted butter over this. Bake at 300 degrees for 30 minutes.

*Mary S. Moss, Washington, North Carolina*

# Broccoli Cheese Casserole

| | | | |
|---|---|---|---|
| 2 | packages chopped broccoli | 3/4 | cup celery, chopped |
| 3/4 | cup onion, chopped | 2 | cans cream of celery soup |
| 1 | stick margarine | 1 | small box instant rice |
| 1 | cup Cheese Whiz | | (2 cups) |

Thaw broccoli. Mix completely with other ingredients. Cover, and bake at 350 degrees for 1 hour.

## Marinated Broccoli and Cauliflower

| | | | |
|---|---|---|---|
| 4 | stalks broccoli | 1 | head cauliflower |
| 3 | stalks celery, diced | 1 | green pepper, diced |
| 1 | onion, diced | 1 1/2 | cups oil |
| 1/2 | cup vinegar | 1 | cup sugar |
| 2 | teaspoons dry mustard | 1 | teaspoon salt |
| 1 | Tablespoon poppy seeds | | |

Cut broccoli and cauliflower into bite-size pieces. Mix broccoli, cauliflower, celery, pepper, and onion. Toss. Combine remaining ingredients, and pour over top of vegetable mixture. Refrigerate overnight. Serves 10 to 12.

## Ladies' Cabbage

Boil a firm, white cabbage, fifteen minutes; change the water and continue boiling until tender, then strain and set aside until perfectly cold; then chop fine, and add two beaten eggs, a tablespoon of butter, three tablespoonfuls of rich milk or cream, a little pepper and salt; stir all well together, and bake in a buttered pudding dish until brown. This dish is digestible and palatable, much resembling cauliflower.

## Harvard Beets

| | | | |
|---|---|---|---|
| 1 | can beets | 1/2 | cup sugar |
| 1/2 | Tablespoon cornstarch | 1/4 | cup vinegar |
| 1/4 | cup beet juice or water | | |

Mix cornstarch and sugar. Add vinegar and juice slowly. Heat slowly, and cook until thickened. Add beets. Cook about 3 minutes.

# Carrot Puff

| | |
|---|---|
| 3 cups mashed carrots | 1/2 cup melted butter or |
| 3 Tablespoons milk | margarine |
| 2 eggs | 2 Tablespoons light brown |
| dash nutmeg | sugar |

Cook carrots in boiling water. Drain. Using a blender or mixer, mash carrots; mix with the melted butter. Add eggs and milk. Mix 1 minute. Add sugar and dash of nutmeg. Mix well, and pour into a greased 1-quart casserole. Bake at 350 degrees for about 30 minutes

# Honey Glazed Carrots

| | |
|---|---|
| 4 1/2 cups carrots (about 2 pounds) | 1 Tablespoon margarine, lite |
| 1 1/2 Tablespoons honey | 1 Tablespoon lemon juice |

Put carrots in vegetable steamer over boiling water. Cover, and steam 4 to 8 minutes. Remove and keep warm. Melt butter in large skillet over medium heat. Add honey and lemon juice, stirring until smooth. Add carrots, and toss gently until coated with sauce.

# Exotic Celery

| | |
|---|---|
| 5 cups celery | 1 can water chestnuts, sliced |
| 1 can cream of chicken soup | 1/2 cup slivered almonds |

Cut celery into medium-sized slices. Drain chestnuts; mix with celery. Place in a 2-quart casserole, and cover with undiluted chicken soup. Sprinkle top with slivered almonds. Bake in a 350 degree oven for 30 minutes.

*Mary S. Moss, Washington, North Carolina*

# Copper Pennies

| | |
|---|---|
| 5 cups sliced carrots, cooked or canned | 1 green pepper, chopped |
| 1 can tomato soup | 1 medium onion, sliced thin, or pearl onions may be used |
| 1/2 cup salad oil | 1 cup sugar |
| 3/4 cup vinegar | 1 teaspoon salt |
| 1 teaspoon pepper | |

Drain carrots. Combine tomato soup, oil, sugar, vinegar, salt, and pepper. Mix until sugar dissolves, and pour over vegetables. Stir until well mixed. Store covered in refrigerator. Keeps well.

*"Corky" Proffitt Bailey, Pearisburg, Virginia*

# Baked Celery Parmesan

Split celery hearts in half. Place in baking dish; sprinkle to taste with salt and pepper. Dot with butter. Add beef boullion to cover bottom of dish. Bake in 375 degree oven for 20 minutes. Baste a few times during baking. Sprinkle generously with Parmesan cheese, and bake 10 minutes longer. Garnish with paprika.

 # Sweet Corn

If some of the tenderest and nicest of the husks are put into a kettle in which corn on the cob is cooked, the flavor of the corn will be improved. Corn is sometimes cooked with the inner husks on, and these are removed just before serving.

# Corn Pudding

Our three sons were raised in a household where everyone helped do all of the chores. They learned many of the skills needed to keep the home fires burning and now use them in their own daily lives. Once, while visiting our son Stephen, we found him getting cupcake batter ready for the oven while keeping watch over a vat on top of the stove that contained bubbling dye for tie-dyeing T-shirts. Both the cupcakes and the dye were to be used at a school activity later in the day involving a club at Kellam High School in Virginia Beach where his wife, Jennifer, was an art teacher. M.P.

| | | | |
|---|---|---|---|
| 1 | can cream style corn | 2 | eggs |
| 2/3 | cup milk | 2 | Tablespoons cornstarch |
| 2 | Tablespoons sugar | 1/2 | teaspoon salt |
| | butter | | |

In a bowl, combine corn, eggs, sugar, and salt. Dissolve cornstarch in milk, and blend into egg mixture. Pour into greased 1-quart casserole. Dot top with butter. Bake uncovered in a 375 degree oven for 45 minutes or so.

*Stephen Proffitt, Virginia Beach, Virginia*

 **Stewed Corn**

Cut fresh corn twice with very sharp knife. Do not slice too close to the cob. Put small amount of water in the pan. Add 1 teaspoon bacon grease (keeps corn from sticking to the pan). When water boils, add corn. Cook slowly, stirring frequently - about 20 minutes. Add salt, pepper, and butter to taste.

# Onion Pie

3  large Bermuda onions
2  eggs
1  prepared pie shell

1/2  stick butter
1/4  cup Parmesan cheese
    bacon, cooked and crumbled

Slice onions, and slowly cook uncovered in butter for about 30 minutes; stir occasionally. Beat eggs with the cheese. Drain onion. Pour eggs and cheese over onions. Pour all into pie shell. Cook in a 300 to 350 degree oven for 20 to 30 minutes. Sprinkle cooked bacon on top when pie comes out of the oven.

*Mary S. Moss, Washington, North Carolina*

# Onion Ormoloo

Peel ten or twelve large white onions, steep them an hour in cold water, then boil them soft. Mash them with an equal quantity of boiled white potatoes, adding half a pint of milk and two or three well beaten eggs. Stir the mixture very hard, season it with nutmeg, pepper and salt, and bake it in a quick oven; when half done pour a little melted butter or gravy over the top.

# Green Peas

Shell green peas until you have a quart; half a peck in the shells will generally produce a quart of shelled peas. Put boiling water to cover them, add a teaspoonful of salt, cover the stew-pan, and boil fast for half an hour; then take one between your fingers; if it will mash easily, they are done: drain off the water, take them into a deep dish; put to them a teacup or less of sweet butter and a little pepper; a small teaspoonful of white sugar is a great improvement. Serve hot. Small young potatoes, nicely scraped, may be boiled and served with them, or in a separate dish with a little butter over.

# Peas and Celery

2 Tablespoons butter
1 3-ounce can mushrooms
2 Tablespoons onion
1/4 teaspoon savory
1 1-pound can peas, drained or
10-ounce package frozen peas,
cooked and drained

1/2 cup celery
2 Tablespoons pimentos
1/2 teaspoon salt
dash pepper

Cut celery on bias; chop pimentos and onions. Melt butter in skillet. Add celery, onions, mushrooms, pimentos, salt, savory, and pepper. Cook uncovered until celery is crisp-done — 5 to 7 minutes. Add drained peas, and heat. Can be made ahead and heated at serving time. Makes 4 nice servings.

# Scalloped Potatoes

6 medium potatoes
1 pint cottage cheese
butter

1 pint sour cream
1 medium onion
sharp yellow cheese, grated

Peel potatoes, and cut in wedges. Cook a short time — do not overcook — and drain. Finely chop onion, and sauté in butter. Pour over potatoes. Mix sour cream and cottage cheese into potatoes. Put in casserole; top with grated cheese. Bake 20 minutes at 350 degrees. Serves 6 to 8.

 # Baking Potatoes

To bake potatoes more quickly, put them in hot water about 15 minutes before placing them in the oven.

# Red Cabbage

Here is another treat from our friend Gerda who cooks such delicious German food.  M.P.

| | | | |
|---|---|---|---|
| 2 | pounds red cabbage | 3 to 4 | Tablespoons red wine |
| | salt | | vinegar |
| 3 | Tablespoons margarine | 1/2 | onion |
| 1 | apple, sour | 1 | teaspoon sugar |
| | water | 1 | Tablespoon flour |
| | spurt of red wine | | |

Remove outer leaves of cabbage, and grind the rest as for cole slaw.  Add vinegar and salt, and mix well.  (This can be done a day ahead.)  Finely chop the onion and sauté in hot margarine.  Add the cabbage, and sauté it until it is somewhat tender.  Add a little water, halved apple, and sugar.  Cover pot, and let cabbage simmer for about 1 and 1/2 hours.  Make a paste with the flour, and add it to the cabbage; simmer another 5 to 10 minutes.  Add wine last.  Delicious!

*Gerda L'Heureux, Virginia Beach, Virginia*

# Potato Casserole

| | | | |
|---|---|---|---|
| 1 | can cream of celery soup | 1/2 | cup milk |
| | dash of pepper and paprika | 1 | small onion, thinly sliced |
| 4 | cups potatoes, thinly sliced | | butter |

Blend soup, milk, and seasonings.  In a 1 1/2-quart casserole, alternate layers of onions, potatoes, and soup mixture.  Dot with butter.  Cover, and bake 1 hour at 375 degrees.  Uncover, and bake for another 15 minutes.

# Cheesed Potatoes

| | |
|---|---|
| 8 small potatoes, unpeeled | 1/4 cup butter |
| 1/2 cup American Cheddar cheese | 1/2 teaspoon salt |
| speck of white pepper | parsley |
| chives | paprika |

Boil potatoes in jackets. Melt butter, and add the grated cheese, salt, and pepper. Peel potatoes quickly; return to saucepan, uncovered. Shake pan gently for a minute or two over burner turned to low heat. This makes the potatoes dry and mealy. Place in a hot serving dish, and pour the butter and cheese mixture over them. Garnish with chopped parsley or chives and paprika. Makes 4 servings.

*Mary S. Moss, Washington, North Carolina*

# Sweet Potato Casserole

| | |
|---|---|
| 3 cups sweet potatoes | 1 cup white sugar |
| 1/2 teaspoon salt | 2 eggs |
| 1/2 stick margarine | 1/2 cup milk |
| 1/2 teaspoon vanilla | |

Mash sweet potatoes. Beat eggs; mix in all other ingredients, and blend into sweet potatoes. Pour into buttered ovenproof dish.

**Topping:**

| | |
|---|---|
| 1/2 stick margarine | 1 cup brown sugar |
| 1/2 cup flour | |

Melt margarine, and combine with sugar and flour. Sprinkle on top of potatoes. Bake in a 350 degree oven for 30 minutes.

*Mae Hogan Proffitt, Roanoke, Virginia*

# Stuffed Potatoes

Our nephew Bruce Proffitt is owner of a wonderful restaurant in Low Moor, Virginia, near Clifton Forge. Several impromptu family gatherings have been held there, relatives have dropped in during deer season, and in 1995, Bruce and his sister, Corky, hosted a spectacular 50th wedding anniversary party there for their parents. Recently, Bruce sent us a copy of this delicious potato recipe for our book, but if you ever visit his restaurant, be sure to save room for the banana fritters with chocolate or butterscotch topping. It's such a specialty at the Cat & Owl that we didn't dare ask him to share that secret with us. M.P.

|  |  |
|---|---|
| 4 large baking potatoes | 1/2 cup margarine |
| 1/2 cup sour cream | 1 1/2 cups sharp Cheddar cheese, |
| 1/2 cup real bacon bits | grated |
| 1/4 cup chives | |

Bake potatoes in a 425 degree oven for 1 hour. Remove from oven, and wrap in foil. Cut potatoes in half lengthwise, and remove insides with a tablespoon. Mix 3/4 cup of the cheese and rest of the ingredients together, and put into potato shell halves. Spread remaining 3/4 cup of cheese on top of potatoes. Return to oven for 2 minutes or until cheese has melted.

*Bruce Proffitt, Cat & Owl Steak and Seafood House, Low Moor, Virginia*

# Hayman Sweet Potatoes

Freshen potatoes by soaking in cold water overnight. Bake in 350 degree oven. Put damp towel over them after they are baked. May be frozen, unpeeled, in a plastic bag.

# Sweet Potato-Bacon Boats

6 to 8 medium sweet potatoes
4 Tablespoons butter or margarine
6 slices bacon, fried

1 cup shredded natural Cheddar cheese
1 teaspoon salt

Scrub potatoes, and bake in a 350 degree oven until done. Cut slice from top of each potato and scoop out the inside. Be careful not to break the shell. In mixing bowl, combine potatoes, shredded cheese, butter or margarine, salt, and a small dash of pepper. Beat until fluffy; fold in crumbled bacon bits, and pile mixture into potato shells. Bake at 350 degrees for 25 to 30 minutes. Top with additional cheese and bacon if desired.

# Spiced Sweet Potatoes

8 large sweet potatoes
1 teaspoon grated orange rind
1/4 cup brown sugar
1/2 teaspoon ground cloves

3/4 cup cream
1 teaspoon salt
1 teaspoon cinnamon
1 to 2 oranges, in segments

Boil potatoes in salted water. Drain, and mash until light. Add cream; beat well. Combine orange rind, salt, brown sugar, cinnamon, and cloves, and add potatoes, mixing well. Spoon individual servings onto 2 lightly greased cookie sheets. Store until ready to use. Remove from refrigerator 1 hour before using. Put orange segment on each, dust with brown sugar, and dot with butter. Bake for 30 minutes in a 400 degree oven. Makes 12 to 15 portions.

# Sweet Potato Soufflé

The ingredients in this dish can be easily divided or multiplied, and have been many times. I got it from a friend when our offsprings were actively involved in young peoples' church activities. I have lost track of my church friend but think of her whenever I pull out the card on which she wrote this recipe. M.P.

| | | | |
|---|---|---|---|
| 2 | large cans sweet potatoes | 3/4 | cup sugar |
| 1 | cup milk | 3/4 | stick margarine |
| 1 | teaspoon vanilla | | |

Heat potatoes; drain, and mash. Add margarine, sugar, milk, and vanilla. Pour into buttered baking dish and add topping.

**Topping:**

| | | | |
|---|---|---|---|
| 1/4 | cup melted margarine | 3 | Tablespoons flour |
| 3/4 | cup light brown sugar | 1/2 | cup pecans, chopped |

Mix ingredients and sprinkle over potatoes. Bake for 30 minutes in a 350 degree oven.

*Mary Hyde, formerly of Virginia Beach, Virginia*

# Peach-Potato Puffs

| | | | |
|---|---|---|---|
| 2 | cups sweet potatoes | 1 | teaspoon lemon juice |
| 2 | Tablespoons brown sugar | 1/4 | teaspoon salt |
| 2 | Tablespoons butter or margarine | 6 | canned peach halves |
| | | | scant dash ground cloves |

Combine mashed sweet potatoes, lemon juice, brown sugar, salt, cloves, and butter or margarine. Whip until fluffy. Arrange peaches in greased 10x6x2-inch baking dish, and pile with potato mixture. Dot with additional butter. Bake for 20 minutes in a 400 degree oven. Makes 6 servings.

# Curried Rice

| | |
|---|---|
| 1  cup rice | 1  Tablespoon curry powder |
| salt | 1  3-ounce can mushrooms |
| 1  package frozen peas | 2  Tablespoons butter |
| 1  Tablespoon pimento | |

Cook rice with curry powder and salt; add drained mushrooms.  Cook peas. Drain, and add to rice along with the butter and pimento.  Mix, and serve while hot.

# Harriett's Rice Curry

| | |
|---|---|
| 1  cup rice, cooked | 4  tomatoes, sliced |
| salt and pepper | 4  eggs, hard boiled |
| grated sharp, or Parmesan | 3  medium onions, sliced |
| cheese | light margarine |
| 1  teaspoon curry powder | flour |
| 1  cup milk | cream |

Slice tomatoes, and arrange in bottom of buttered casserole.  Add salt and pepper. Place sliced eggs over tomatoes.  Sprinkle on a little salt.  Spread grated cheese over this.  Fry onions in a little butter, and, when soft, add curry powder.  Add a little flour to this mixture; stir until smooth, and add milk to make sauce.  Pour sauce over casserole; spread rice on top.  Pour a little cream on top of rice.  Bake about 30 minutes in a 350 degree oven.  Cover with greased foil to prevent sticking.

# Spinach Casserole

3  10-ounce packages chopped spinach
6  Tablespoons butter
   pepper
   grated rind of 1 lemon

3  3-ounce packages cream cheese
   salt
   nutmeg
1  cup packaged herb dressing

Cook spinach according to directions.  Drain, and return to hot saucepan.  Blend in cream cheese, butter, salt, pepper, nutmeg, and lemon rind.  Turn into buttered casserole.  Cover, and refrigerate until ready to bake.  45 minutes before baking, remove from refrigerator and spread dry herb dressing over top.  Bake at 350 degrees for 20 minutes.  Serves 8.

*Mary Stewart Darden, Virginia Beach, Virginia*

# Squash with Water Chestnuts

2  pounds squash
1  can cream of shrimp soup
   toasted bread crumbs

1  large onion
1  can water chestnuts
   butter

Cut squash in 1/2-inch thick slices.  Dice onion, and sauté in a little butter.  Mix squash and onion with soup.  Drain, and thinly slice water chestnuts; stir into soup mixture.  Spoon into casserole, and top with toasted bread crumbs.  Bake in preheated 350 degree oven for 15 minutes.  Do not overcook.  Squash should be crisp and crunchy.  (A can of cream of celery may be substituted for the cream of shrimp soup.)

*Mary S. Moss, Washington, North Carolina*

# Squash Casserole

| | |
|---|---|
| 3 to 4 cups squash, cooked | 2 eggs, beaten |
| 1 medium onion, chopped | 1 cup milk |
| buttered bread crumbs | salt and pepper |

Slice yellow squash, and cook with chopped onion in a small amount of boiling salted water until tender. Drain and mash. Add beaten eggs which have been mixed with the milk. Season with salt and pepper, and pour into buttered casserole. Bake in a 350 degree oven for about 45 minutes. Add buttered crumbs on top for the last few minutes of cooking.

*Mary S. Moss, Washington, North Carolina*

# Baked Tomatoes

Ray Baker was on the faculty at Lynnhaven Elementary School when Mary and I taught there. She was young and energetic, and a favorite of both students and fellow teachers. M.P.

| | |
|---|---|
| 2 cans tomatoes | 2 cups sugar |
| 1 stick margarine | 4 to 6 slices stale bread |
| 1 1/2 teaspoons cinnamon | |

Blend tomatoes, sugar, and bread pieces in baking dish. Top with pats of margarine, and sprinkle with cinnamon. Bake in a 400 degree oven for 45 minutes.

*Ray "Razor" Baker, Lynnhaven Elementary School Staff,*
*1960's, Virginia Beach, Virginia*

Where are you, Ray?

# Asparagus au Gratin

Arrange cooked asparagus (fresh, canned, or frozen) on baking sheet. Dot with butter or margarine; sprinkle with salt and pepper. Top lavishly with grated Parmesan cheese. Place in broiler with surface of food about 4 inches below heat. Broil until cheese browns lightly.

# Easy String Beans

Drain one can of French-style string beans, add 2 teaspoons of dry onion soup mix. Place in small pan. Top with one strip of uncooked bacon, diced. Bake in 400 degree oven until bacon is done.

# Almond Green Beans

| | |
|---|---|
| 1/4 cup slivered almonds | 1/4 cup butter |
| 1/4 teaspoon salt | 1 to 2 teaspoons lemon juice |
| 2 cups French-style green beans | |

Cook almonds in butter over low heat until golden, stirring occasionally. Remove from heat; add salt and lemon juice. Pour over cooked, drained green beans. Serves 4.

 # Sugar and Salt

Add a pinch of sugar to everything sour or salty. Add a pinch of salt to coffee and everything sweet. It helps to bring out its flavor.

# Fresh Green Beans

| | |
|---|---|
| 1 pound fresh green beans | 2 to 3 Tablespoons butter or |
| 1/2 cup onion, chopped | margarine |
| 1/4 cup celery, chopped | 1 clove garlic, minced |
| 1/4 teaspoon rosemary, crushed | 1/4 teaspoon basil, crushed |
| salt | |

Cut beans in 1-inch lengths. Cover, and cook in boiling salted water for 10 minutes; drain. Stir in remaining ingredients. Cover; cook over low heat until tender. Season to taste with salt.

# Zucchini Quiche

| | |
|---|---|
| 2 Tablespoons butter or | 1 pound zucchini, chopped |
| margarine | 1/2 cup sliced onion |
| 3/4 teaspoon salt, divided | 1/2 teaspoon oregano |
| 1/4 teaspoon basil | 3/4 cup shredded Swiss cheese |
| 1 baked 9-inch pie shell | 1 1/2 cups half-and-half |
| 1 1/2 teaspoons cornstarch | 3 eggs |
| pinch nutmeg | dash liquid hot pepper sauce |

Melt butter or margarine in a large skillet over medium heat. Add zucchini, onion, 1/2 teaspoon salt, oregano, and basil. Cook and stir until zucchini is tender, about 5 minutes. Increase heat, and continue to cook until moisture is completely evaporated, stirring occasionally. Remove from heat. Toss with cheese, and immediately distribute evenly on bottom of pie shell. In bowl, mix half-and-half with cornstarch. Beat in eggs, nutmeg, hot pepper sauce, and remaining 1/4 teaspoon salt. Pour into pie shell. Bake at 400 degrees until set and lightly browned on top, about 25 minutes. Serve hot or at room temperature. Makes 6 servings.

# Zucchini Casserole

6  cups zucchini, sliced
1  12-ounce can tomatoes
   cracker crumbs
   butter or margarine

2  large onions, sliced
1  teaspoon oregano
   grated cheese

In a little melted butter or margarine, cook zucchini and onions together until tender, but not too soft.  Drain.  Cut up tomatoes, pour into pan with zucchini and onions, add oregano, and mix.  Put a layer of zucchini mixture in bottom of greased baking dish; top with a layer of cracker crumbs and a layer of grated cheese.  Repeat layers until all mixture is used.  Bake for 20 minutes in 300 degree oven.

# Parmesan Baked Potatoes

8  medium unpeeled red
   or white potatoes
3  Tablespoons grated Parmesan
   cheese

6  Tablespoons butter
   or margarine

Cut potatoes in half lengthwise.  Melt butter and pour into a 9x13x2-inch baking dish.  Sprinkle Parmesan cheese over butter.  Place potatoes with cut side down over cheese.  Bake uncovered at 400 degrees for 40 to 45 minutes or until tender.  Serves 8.

*Michelle Bishop Darden, Virginia Beach, Virginia*

# CONTRIBUTORS

Sherry Arendt
"Corky" Proffitt Bailey
Jean Ann Bailey
Ray Baker
Ruth Barco
Bayside Junior High Faculty
Louise Bland
Marguerite Brassell
Central Office, VB Schools
Jane Cheek
Helen Taylor Clark
Josephine Proffitt Clements
Eleanor Cooke
Jim Darden
Michelle Bishop Darden
Joann DeFilippo
Dot Denton
Selma Jean Everett
Janie Proffitt Flippo
Sara S. Gabel
Debby Gooch
June Hand-Decker
Sharon Haring
Augusta Jane Hogan
Meg Heckel
Anne Hopewell
"Pete" Hughey
Mary Hyde
Kempsville High Faculty
Gerda L'Heureux
Elsie Lockhart
Joan Manuel

Dottie McCarson
Nancy McCowen
Sara Moss McCowen
Diane Post Miller
Jeannine Moss
Mary S. Moss
Annie Fox Proffitt
Bruce Proffitt
Don Proffitt
Gail Boyle Proffitt
Genevieve Proffitt
Jeanne Miller Proffitt
Jennifer Taylor Proffitt
Lawrence Proffitt
Leon Proffitt
Mae Hogan Proffitt
Michael Proffitt
"Sis" Waid Proffitt
Stephen Proffitt
Susan Proffitt
Dottie Reynolds
Emily Groover Shelley
Rose Snyder
Annie Harrell Stewart
Helen Stewart
Robert Stewart
Iva Suttles
Alice Heath Taylor
Jean Jordan Taylor
Michelle Taylor
Judy Ward
Anne Proffitt Wine

# INDEX

241